2

The Netball Coaching Manual

j

The Netball Coaching Manual

Edited by Heather Crouch

A & C Black • London

Published by A & C Black (Publishers) Ltd
35 Bedford Row, London WC1R 4JH

Second edition, in paperback, 1992
Reprinted 1995
First edition 1984

ISBN 0 7136 3530 4

A CIP catalogue record for this book
is available from the British Library

Designed by Douglas Martin Associates
Line illustration by John Dillow
Cover photograph by Eileen Langsley

Printed and bound in Great Britain by
The Bath Press, Avon

Contents

Acknowledgements

My sincere thanks to:

all contributors for responding so graciously to my editorial comments and producing such stimulating chapters for this book;

the A E N A Coaching Committee for their trust in leaving me to produce this manual for the association;

the photographers, Eileen Langsley, Jergen Hasenkopf, Brian Worrell, Bill Hickey, Lynn Turner and Robin Cuisick, for their patience, time and excellent results;

the England and Essex Wanderers players and the students of the Anglia Polytechnic who gave their time to be photographed;

Brenda Tooley, to whom we all owe a debt of gratitude for typing and retyping the scripts and final drafts – it has been a delight to work with someone so tolerant, helpful and efficient;

Sylvia Eastley for her assistance;

Gordon Padley for his advice;

Gordon Crouch for his patience and understanding; and

a special thanks to the National Westminster Bank for their support.

Heather Crouch

Key

The authors have used the following conventions throughout:

⟶ line of the ball

– – – – –► player running

–|–|–|– |–► player repositioning

× player

Ⓧ defending player

Introduction

This book is intended as a reference for all those interested in netball coaching. Indeed, it is hoped that coaches of other sports may also find some of the chapters relevant to them. Each chapter has been written by an expert in that particular field and can be read as a self-contained unit, although an overall coherence throughout the book should also be evident. It is hoped that the pooled knowledge of the twelve contributors produces a comprehensive coaching manual. The aim has been to provide a text that will stimulate thoughts and ideas about coaching and enhance the standards of netball playing.

Heather Crouch

Chapter 1

The game of netball

Joyce Wheeler

Joyce Wheeler is a former lecturer at the Chelsea School of Human Movement, Brighton Polytechnic. She is an Advanced coach and International umpire. She is an ex-England Captain, and has also been England Coach (1975–79). She was the National Development Officer for the A E N A from 1973 to 1978, and is now an England selector. She has tutored numerous coaching and umpiring courses both in the UK and abroad. She is the author of two books on netball.

THE BASIC CONCEPTS OF THE GAME

Netball is a fast, enjoyable and skilful game in which people of all ages and levels of ability may participate. Its requirements are simple: a hard well lit surface covering an area of 30.5m (100ft) × 15.25m (50ft) (see Figure 1), two netball posts 3.05m (10ft) high each with a ring 380mm (15in) in diameter, a size 5 ball, fourteen players, two umpires and, ideally, a coach.

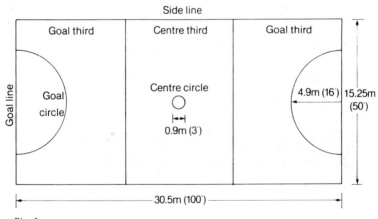

Fig. 1

The game involves a variety of ways of passing the ball successfully from one team member to another, so that a goal may be scored from within the shooting circle by throwing the ball through the ring. All seven players in the team have an equal part to play in achieving this aim, and at some stage will need to defend and to attack. This obviously demands a variety of skills and the ability of each player to be selective in the use of them, so as to produce a flowing, energetic and stimulating game. The players need to be quick-thinking, as they are required to make speedy and accurate decisions on the ever-changing situations presented to them.

The skills needed in netball include landing, pivoting, changing direction, stopping, starting, throwing, catching, getting free, marking, intercepting and shooting. Players need spatial awareness of (a) themselves, (b) the court and (c) the team. These are individual skills which must be learned and then applied as in the open game situation. The application of these skills will be used as tactics in the game. These issues will be dealt with more fully in later chapters.

THE RULES OF THE GAME

Obviously the rules impose certain limitations on the game and on how it is played. The size of the playing area imposes spatial limitations generally, and every player has limitations placed upon them by the specific position in which they play (see Figure 2).

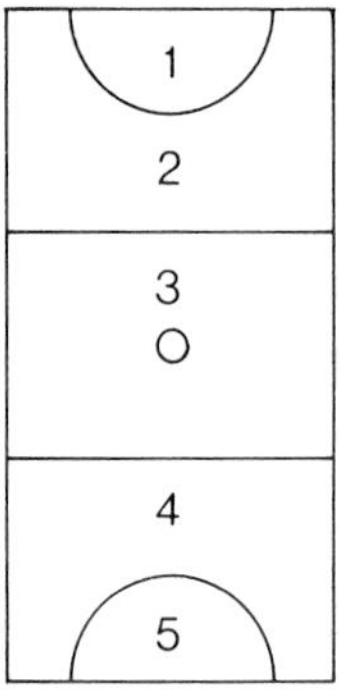

Position	Area
GS (Goal Shooter)	1, 2
GA (Goal Attack)	1, 2, 3
WA (Wing Attack)	2, 3
C (Centre)	2, 3, 4
WD (Wing Defence)	3, 4
GD (Goal Defence)	3, 4, 5
GK (Goal Keeper)	4, 5

Fig. 2 Playing areas

Starting and restarting the game

Every game has a different method of starting and in netball this is achieved by each centre taking a centre pass.

The game commences with all players in their allotted areas (see Figure 3; the arrow indicates the direction of play). The centre with the ball must be wholly in the centre circle. All other players are free to move within their own playing area. On the whistle the Goal Attack (GA), Wing Attack (WA), Wing Defence (WD) and Goal Defence (GD) may move into the centre third (i.e., area B) to receive the first pass. The ball is then passed until it is received in a suitable position in the shooting circle.

Once a goal has been scored, the ball returns to the centre and the pass is taken by the team who did not take the previous centre pass.

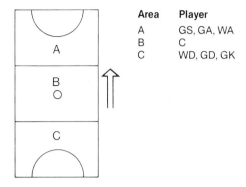

Area	Player
A	GS, GA, WA
B	C
C	WD, GD, GK

Fig. 3 Areas allocated to players before the start of play

Playing positions

As well as an all-round ability, netball demands specialisation. Each player has a specific role to play, and the emphasis is put on either attacking or defending skill. Some players have a more natural tendency to attack while others enjoy the challenge of defence. Within these two general categories there is another division:

○ 2 shooters (attackers)
○ 3 centre-court players (attackers and defenders)
○ 2 defenders

These seven players constitute a team.

Each player has specific responsibilities (see Chapter 13), and both the player and the coach should be aware of them, so that (a) the player can carry out her role efficiently and effectively and (b) the coach can make appropriate selection for a successful and harmonious team.

EQUIPMENT

So far as clothing is concerned, netball places few demands upon the players or officials.

The *players* are required to have suitable clothing in which to move freely and safely. Players are requested to wear the initials of their position – 20cm (8in) high – both front and back above the waist on their playing uniform. Correct footwear, i.e., shoes or lightweight boots, must be worn. The soles should be free of spikes. For the safety of all players, no jewellery may be worn with the exception of wedding rings, which must be taped.

Umpires need to keep warm but must also realise the importance of free movement; therefore a tracksuit and/or a lightweight anorak should be worn. Suitable footwear should be worn. Other requirements are a whistle on a cord, a watch with a second hand, a scorecard (where applicable), a copy of the current AENA rules, a ballpoint pen and a pencil.

If there are official *scorers* and *timekeepers*, they have certain requirements: a table, a score pad, pens and a bell – to stop the game if the wrong centre pass is taken. Timekeepers need two stop watches and a whistle.

Playing equipment

The requirements are (a) a hard surface, (b) two netball posts, and (c) a ball.

A hard surface which must be non-slip, porous, resilient, hard-wearing and level is necessary.

The court markings are usually painted lines, but care should be taken to ensure they are not slippery when it rains. Indoors adhesive or plastic coated tape may be used. The lines should be 50mm (2in) wide, and it is recommended that they should be yellow.

The goal-posts should be 3.05m (10ft) high with a tubular steel ring of 380mm (15in) diameter projecting horizontally 150mm (6in) from the top of the post. The ring should have a nylon or twine net open at both ends. The base may be inserted into a socket in the ground or supported by a metal base which does not project onto the court. Some posts are on wheels, which makes transportation easier. The bases must provide stability.

A netball or association football size 5 is used; it should be made of leather, rubber or similar material. It should weigh between 400g (14oz) and 450g (16oz), and should be between 660mm (27in) and 710mm (28in) in circumference.

Changing accommodation

Adequate facilities should be available and easily accessible to the courts and players. They should include changing rooms, showers and refreshment facilities.

Netball is a relatively easy game to initiate, but playing performance and enjoyment are enhanced if players, coaches, umpires and other officials are fully conversant with the rules. Rule books are available from the AENA Head Office.

Chapter 2
The basic skills of netball
Gerry Cornwell

Gerry Cornwell is the Financial Director of Weathercock Properties.
She is an Advanced Coach and Umpire, and the President of Bedfordshire
County Netball Association. She was Chairman of the East Region
from 1977 to 1983. She was Assistant England Coach and England
Under 21 Coach from 1985 to 1987. She was also an England selector
for many years.

INTRODUCTION

The basic skills are not just the concern of the beginner coach, they are
an essential part of the understanding and repertoire of all coaches. This
chapter introduces the basic skills and will help to give ideas for successfully
coaching and observing them.

As with all coaching, concepts do not stand still: existing ideas are
adapted and new information is brought into all levels of the game. This
chapter aims to reinforce ideas as well as suggest new thoughts.

A beginner coach usually has to cope in the first instance with one of the
following situations:

○ a group that has never played the game and is learning the basic skills
from the beginning
○ a group that can cope with playing the game but not particularly
skilfully

Coaches who find that their present coaching is with a group like the first
of these should continue reading this chapter at the start of the section on
primary skills (see page 14).

OBSERVATION

Whenever possible, players should be observed playing the game before the
coach decides which of the basic skills to deal with first. Because it is difficult
to observe and to take in all that a game offers, coaches need to be selective in
their observations.

It is often helpful further to subdivide basic skills into two categories:

Primary skills	Secondary skills
O footwork	O getting free
O catching	O marking
O throwing	O shooting
	O throw-up

This subdivision indicates that the primary skills should be learnt first, and that players should be competent in them before progressing to the secondary skills.

How does a coach know when the players are competent? The assessment chart in Figure 4 can be used while observing a game or practice match. If you come out of the 'conclusion' exit then pass on to the section on secondary skills (page 24). However, if your players are not yet totally competent it is appropriate to select one of the primary skills from the section on primary skills. This procedure should be continued until all the primary skills have been dealt with.

PRIMARY SKILLS

Footwork

Footwork is the most essential skill with which to start. From good footwork stems good netball.

In this introductory discussion we are concerned only with the one/two landing.

The stride pattern

When on the move to take the pass, the length of the player's stride – particularly prior to jumping to catch the ball – should be observed. The stride pattern should be even and not too long, and it is preferable to see a shortening of the stride immediately prior to take-off. This should allow for greater elevation.

Elevation

Elevation should be encouraged in the early days of learning footwork. It gives the player the necessary time to select the appropriate landing foot, and is of major benefit in achieving balanced landing and body control.

Body

When in the air, the top half of the body should be upright, not bent forward. This common fault, if not observed and corrected, can be the main cause of imbalance on landing.

The knee of the landing foot should bend on contact with the ground, so as to absorb the impact, and thereby help maintain body stability.

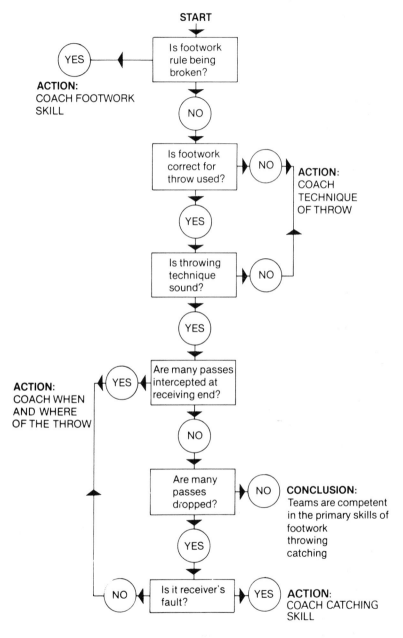

Fig. 4 Assessment chart for primary skills

Landing foot

If a player throws the ball right-handed, then the landing foot should be the *right*; the reverse is true for the left-handed thrower. Contact with the ground is initially with the ball of the foot, but the whole of the foot should have contact if the body weight is correct and over the landing foot.

The placement of the second foot must not be ignored: it should be a comfortable stride width in front of the landing foot. The distance on the ground between the landing foot and the second foot is referred to as the footbase, and for the netballer of average height it is approximately 60cm (2ft). If the body weight is forward and the landing foot not wholly in contact with the ground, there will be a tendency to drag the landing foot and for the player to be penalised for breaking the footwork rule. This unbalanced, wide base can be corrected by employing the second foot as a brake, using short stabbing movements into the ground.

If the braking action is used to gain control, then correction to this wide base, by using short pushing steps to adjust the body position and bring the feet closer together, will now be needed.

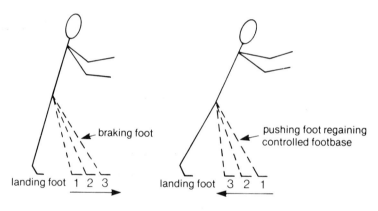

Fig. 5

Pivot

The landing foot – usually the ball of the foot – remains in contact with the ground. The other foot becomes the 'looking' foot and with short pushes propels the body in the required direction.

Both feet should point in the direction of the subsequent pass. The coach should be aware of the shortest way round towards the throwing space, and observe how quickly the player is responding to the need to use the pivot.

If carried out quickly and sharply, the pivot can be a very effective means of avoiding a defender who is attempting to defend the throw of the player with the ball.

Catching

Ball handling

All too often ball handling is ignored in favour of coaching the 'skills'. Yet to make your players ultimately the best, they must feel comfortable handling the ball in adverse conditions at awkward levels of the body and in less than ideal circumstances.

To receive the ball one-handed, the hand should be cupped slightly in a relaxed manner. When the ball makes contact, the palm and the fingers should open to receive the ball. The wrist should be flexible and the arm should give.

Players should practise receiving the ball with either the right or the left hand, high above the head, out wide to the sides (the wings) and down low to the calves and the ankles.

Initially it may be possible to hear a 'smacking' on the ball from less confident and relaxed players. As confidence and the ability to relax increase this will disappear.

Catching

Initially this is a two-handed operation, safe catching being of paramount importance.

A high
two-handed
catch

Ensure that the player is watching the ball right up to the point when it enters the hands. Too often the attention is transferred prematurely to throwing, and the catch becomes unsuccessful.

Where possible, players should be encouraged to jump, stretch and meet the ball early. The fingers should be spread and the hands slightly cupped and not tense. After catching, the thumbs should be at the back of the ball (nearest the body). The hands should be just over half-way down the ball. Snatching the ball into the body to a 'holding' position or into an area away from an opponent should be encouraged until such time as the players become skilful enough to catch and release the ball immediately.

Throwing

Footwork

Correct throwing technique is heavily dependent on correct footwork.

Assuming the one/two landing has been made, the body should now be in a balanced position, with the ball sitting comfortably in both hands in the centre of the body just above the chest.

For any throwing action where the movement is forward, encourage the player to transfer weight from the back landing foot onto the forward 'looking' foot, which should be pointing in the direction of the throw. This transference of weight should be timed to coincide with the thrusting forward of the throwing arm(s).

It might be that the stride is lengthened when carrying this out, and this is quite often the case when a long throw is involved. A common fault when lengthening the stride in order to force the ball a longer distance is that the landing foot is dragged. The coach should be particularly observant in this area.

Throwing stages

There are three phases involved in producing the throw:

Phase 1 (a) holding stage – usually the catching position
(b) preparation stage – taking the ball to the part of the body it is to be released from

Phase 2 (a) point of release – the point at which the ball loses contact with the fingers
(b) flight of ball – the trajectory taken by the ball, influenced by the direction of the arm(s) and fingers

Phase 3 (a) follow through – the action after the moment of release

The 'holding' stage as a deliberate action should be encouraged among beginner players. The coach should be aware of the catching point, when the player is receiving a pass.

As the player becomes more skilful, this stage becomes less easy to perceive, becoming an integral part of the 'catching for release' action. On the assumption that the catching action is to the 'holding' position, preparation of the pass will be initiated from here. When the player is ready to pass, the ball should be whipped from the 'holding' position to the point from which it will ultimately be released. This action ensures that defending players are not given information as to which type of pass is about to be made or from where it will be released.

The coach should be aware of any player who allows the ball to remain for any significant amount of time at the point of release. There is often a tendency for players learning the technique of a shoulder throw to pause prior to releasing the ball. The beginner player needs time for the preparation and for release speed to be developed. However, the coach should attempt to get this timespan shortened, thus maintaining the maximum surprise value of the pass.

The follow through gives direction to the pass, and should not be ignored. In the early days of learning, the coach should encourage players to exaggerate this action, extending through the arms to the tips of the fingers in the direction that the ball is to travel.

When to throw

If the three phases described above can be implemented effectively, then the 'when to throw' becomes easy to judge. Quite simply, the pass is made when the receiver makes the final movement to get free. However, be aware that this is a 'chicken and egg' situation. If the preparation and release action of the thrower cannot be carried out quickly, then the defender will be able to read where the pass is coming from and apply defending pressure to delay it.

The receiver by this time could have been free and subsequently remarked. The solution must come from improving the preparation and release *or* improving the 'getting free' of the receiver (see page 24) and thereby giving more time for release of the ball.

Where to throw

The simple answer to this must be 'to the unmarked space which the receiver can reach before the opposition'. For many short-distance passes, 'where' rather than the height of the pass should be taken as the coaching point to concentrate on. 'Where' is the *free space* into which to put the ball. However, if the receiver is running to goal to receive a long shoulder throw, then the height of the pass is important; above head-height is the ideal place to take the ball, so that the receiver can catch and turn for goal all in one movement. If the pass is a shorter one, then the type of pass often dictates the height at which it is to be received:

O   push pass   approximately shoulder/chest
O   overhead/lob pass   above head of receiver, when either static or
                            jumping
O   bounce pass   knee to waist
O   drop pass   ankle to knee
O   slip/underarm pass   hip

Technique

One-handed shoulder throw: The ball should be lifted and released from shoulder- or head-height. The hand should be behind the ball with the fingers spread. For some players this will be difficult, and the other hand may be needed to help with control. The body should be turned so that the opposite shoulder to the throwing shoulder is pointing in the direction of the throw. With the transference of weight, the pulling round of the hips and the pushing forward of the throwing shoulder, the throw will be made. The arm and then the fingers follow through in the direction of the pass, generating a pass of the required accuracy and force. The coach should be aware of the top half of the player's body at the point of release of the ball. If it is bent forward, then the throwing arm will come round and so affect the ultimate direction and flight of the ball.

Two-handed push pass: This can be made from any part of the upper body. However, players have been encouraged to take the ball to the central body position, and it might be that initially this is where the pass will be released from. The hands should be at the sides of the ball with the fingers pointing in the direction of the pass. The release action involves pushing the ball forward, straightening the elbows as the ball is released, with the fingers making the final push and following through in the direction of the pass. As with the shoulder throw, there can be weight transference, but because long distances are not usually involved body turn is not essential, and neither is the lengthening of the stride.

It should be easy, once the technique has been learned, for the beginner player to develop a push-pass from either side of the body. However, coaches must constantly be aware that players develop favourite passing positions; they should not be allowed to become predictable with regard to the release position.

To make a push pass from the side there is a degree of body turn, and the hands also turn – one on the top, one slightly under. The same pushing action is carried out with the arm and the fingers, following through in the direction of the flight of the ball.

Overhead/lob: This is becoming a specific situation pass. The ball is held above the head with the hands on the sides. Footwork is important for this pass: the base should not be too wide, because stability is critical. A slight transference of weight to the front foot is made as the pass is executed.

If an overhead pass is required (e.g., a throw-in), the ball should be taken back slightly with the wrists cocked. Then, with a forceful movement from the elbow followed through to the fingers, the ball is propelled forward in a high straight-line throw.

If a lob is required, then no backward movement is necessary: the wrists and fingers should cope. The fingers push the ball forward and up. With this pass it is critical that they are worked and extended until the ball is released.

The flight of the ball and where it is ultimately received can differ depending upon the requirement of the situation. For example, if it is to go into the receiver's hands at the highest point possible, above any defending player, the flight path must remain high, so that the ball is ultimately snatched out of the air by the attacking player. On the other hand, 'over and

The lob pass,
showing the action
of fingers and wrists

The lob pass,
showing finger and
wrist action of the
thrower and high
receiving position of
the GS (see Figure 6)

beyond' suggests that the flight of the ball is at its highest point *beyond* the attacker, dropping sharply so that the attacker can turn into the pass (Figure 6).

The lob is regarded as a 'feel' pass, and it will take time before learners can execute it effectively, particularly as a feed to a shooter in a confined space (Figure 7).

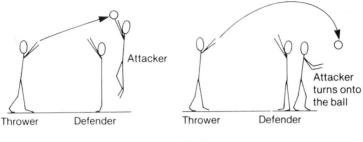

Fig. 6   Fig. 7

Underarm/slip pass: The ball is taken onto one hand at approximately hip-height. There is an exaggerated transference of weight onto the front foot, with the knee being bent to avoid dragging the landing foot. The arm is pushed forward, allowing the ball to roll along the open hand, with the final push being given by the fingers. The arm and hand then follow through in the direction of the pass. This is a very simple pass and players should be able to execute it from either hand.

Bounce/drop pass: This is often the pass with which to catch out a defender. It can be executed from one or both hands. For two-handed bounce or drop passes (as with the push pass), the hands are at the sides of the ball.

Weight is transferred onto the front foot as the pass is made, so that the thrower is often taken close to the defender. In order to get the ball under the defender, the knees should be slightly bent and the ball released so as to bounce past the defender's feet. It should be directed downwards fiercely as it is to be received by a player in an upright position.

For the one-handed bounce or drop pass, the fingers are spread with the hand under and behind the ball. Body weight is transferred as for the two-handed pass. The use of one hand means that less force can be directed into the pass and, as there is also less control, accuracy can suffer. Distance now becomes critical and, since the force applied is less, only shorter distances should be contemplated. However, a wider choice of points of release is now possible, and opportunities to try to 'bend' the ball around the defender are offered.

If the defender to be beaten is marking the receiver, and the thrower sees a close space that the defender cannot reach, then a 'drop' bounce pass can be made. It is necessary to step into this pass with an exaggerated bending of the knees, pushing the ball very slightly towards the ground into the space *protected* by the receiver. This type of pass should not rise off the ground more than 30cm (1ft), so that the defender is given little or no chance of intercepting it.

SECONDARY SKILLS

Getting free

Many aspects of play have to be knitted together to 'get free'. The manoeuvre cannot be carried out in isolation from other players, and it should always be a related exercise. A thrower ready to release the ball and a receiver available to take a pass are the two component parts which can be worked on independently, but ultimately they must be welded together.

Aspects of getting free include

○   readiness
○   technique – sudden sprint and change of direction
○   timing
○   where
○   final movement

Readiness

Readiness is a state all players are in throughout the match. Weight should be evenly distributed, with the feet comfortably apart (approximately shoulder-width). Knees should be flexed and the body bent slightly forward, with the weight over the balls of the feet.

Technique

There are two basic techniques for getting free:

Sprint: For this to be effective, speed must be implemented as quickly as possible. To obtain sudden speed, the feet and body should be pointing in the required direction, and the weight should be over the leading foot so that the player feels almost overbalanced. The coach should continually check the time taken by the player to get from a state of readiness to a full-speed movement. This time should, for the good player, be minimal and, in terms of court distance, no more than two or three strides. The longer in both time and distance it takes for the sprint speed to be implemented, the more opportunity is given to the defender to react and catch the attacking player. The coach should ensure that the player is not looking at her feet or bent over, as though running in a race, prior to starting a sprint.

Change of direction: This involves taking an opponent in one direction and then, with a sudden braking movement of the leading foot, changing direction. If the first such change does not result in getting freedom, then another change of direction should be made, and so on until a successful result is obtained. The coach should watch the technique of the direction change and help the player improve so that a single commitment is enough to obtain freedom.

If the direction change is not sudden enough, and does not result in freedom, the coach should check that the knee of the braking foot bends, and that the body weight does not go over this foot. It is the bending of the knee that absorbs the pace of movement prior to the change, and it is the spring from which the change of direction comes. However, having once established that the player is not dithering, the coach should encourage players to play with speed and multiple direction change, to find an effective method for getting free.

Timing

Perhaps one of the hardest components to coach and maintain is timing. Players should be in a state of readiness, waiting for the cue or cues which indicate when to get free. They must become used to observing and responding. Practice stimuli to which to respond could be the dropping or picking up of a ball. In a game, the main cue will be the moment that the thrower is ready and able to pass the ball. Once the cue is received, movement such as a sprint may be introduced.

It is important to stress that all players are individuals, and that a cue from one player will not necessarily be the same as one from the next. Many combinations should be tried, allowing players to take cues from many different colleagues. Timing can be likened to the coiling of a spring – it is wound up, and then released at the most effective time. The player getting free should make the final movement *when the thrower is ready to release the ball.*

Where

The ball should be thrown *into the free space,* and this can be difficult for the coach to pinpoint because of a defender limiting the movement of an

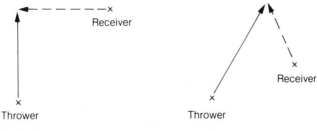

Fig. 8a Correct   Fig. 8b Incorrect, receiver running away

attacking player. The receiver should ideally try to meet the ball at a right angle, or even at an angle towards the thrower (Figure 8).

Initially the receiver should not be allowed to run away from the thrower until accuracy and passing techniques have been fully mastered. Encourage the receiver to aid the thrower by indicating with the hand where the ball is to be received. The hand can show the height of the pass as well as the direction.

Final movement

Any method of getting free must involve positive and total commitment to taking the ball. Strides should be kept slightly short until the final lunge or jump is made to take the ball: this assists controlled landing. Work for speed and elevation from the players. When and where possible they should end up, with the ball, facing towards their goal.

Defending

The first stage of man-to-man marking is described here. It is the method of marking that attempts to achieve

O   an interception of the pass if it is made
O   the covering of an opponent's movements, making her unusable

The defender should take up a position in front of the attacker with the back of either her right or left shoulder centred on the opponent's body. Some defenders prefer to remain parallel to their opponent while others prefer to turn inwards slightly, thus marking at an angle. Both can be tried to see which is the more effective for any particular player.

The defender should be in a state of readiness and able to shadow easily any movement made by the attacker. She also needs to be aware of any pass made to her opponent. It is necessary to keep a compact footbase, in order to achieve instant elevation or, to stretch outwards should a pass be made, stride extension. Recovery from being sent the wrong way will also be quicker if the stride width is kept compact.

The coach should continually monitor the shadowing of an opponent, ensuring that contact is not made and that a large gap does not develop between defender and opponent. A defender in this situation should be aware

The first stage of defence is to intercept the ball

of the length of time in terms of staying with an opponent for more than three seconds. When the defender perceives the thrower and tightens her marking, she should stay aware of the pass time being eroded due to her good marking.

If a coach wishes to encourage interception, then the defender can invite the pass to her opponent by relaxing her shadow marking just enough for the thrower to think it is possible to make a pass. The defender's total readiness would then be committed to interception. A fault of many defenders when going for interception is that, after they have taken the ball, contact is made with the opponent and a penalty is given against them. Once players have learnt to intercept at an angle, cutting the ball off slightly earlier, the possibility of contact is reduced (Figure 9).

Fig. 9a Straight line

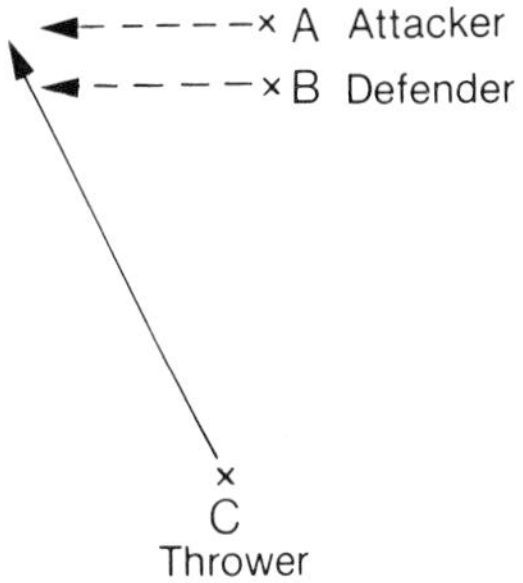

×A Attacker
×B Defender

×
C
Thrower

Fig. 9b Angled

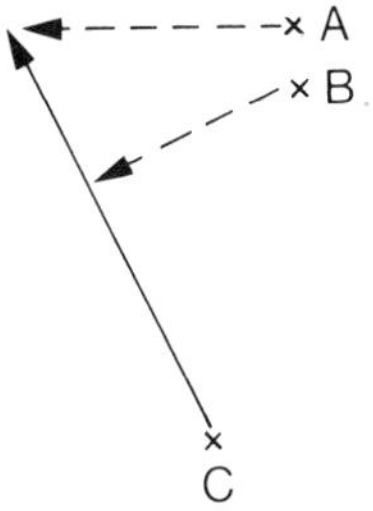

×A
×B

×
C

Shooting

Whether shooters are 'born' or 'made' can be argued indefinitely. However, without good scoring in the circle, games will be lost. Shooting is a relatively closed skill and can be practised in total isolation from the rest of the team.

To obtain consistently high shooting percentages, practice is strongly recommended. For the beginner, the static shot needs to be learnt. The footbase should be stable, with both feet on the ground; the leading foot should preferably be the landing foot. The other foot should be placed behind or close to it so that a comfortable stance is taken up. The weight should be over the back foot, with the knee of this back leg bent. A coach should encourage her shooters to practise with either foot leading so that the action of pulling back onto the back foot is possible in all situations.

The point of release of the ball to goal should be as high as is comfortable, with the ball sitting on the flat of the hand; the other hand may be used to aid control. The coach should be watchful for a shooter whose action starts high but who lowers the ball when preparing to release the shot. The target aimed for should be the back of the ring, so that the shooter has the incentive to lift the ball over the front.

The shooting rhythm that should develop will differ according to the distance from the post. It will be more exaggerated on the outer edge of the circle. The further away from the ring, the more push that is required, so that the knees must bend more, and the arms work by pushing up with eventually the fingers following *up* and *over*, releasing the ball to goal. The shooter should be consistent with her action even when a defender is present. Shooters should be carefully watched to see if changes of action under pressure occur, since this can be the main cause of loss of accuracy during a match.

Toss-up

All players should be competent at this skill. When taking up the position facing goal, the forward foot should be furthest away from the umpire, thus opening up the body to the ball. The ball should be watched all the time as it is being put into the space by the umpire. Knees should be

slightly bent and the hands relaxed at the sides of the body. When the whistle is blown, the aim is to snatch the ball away from the area and turn the body to protect it. Beginners may need to take a second or so to assess the situation before releasing the ball.

Too often successful throw-ups become unsuccessful passes because the supporting players have not reacted to the new attacking situation. If a player is not successful, she must be encouraged to defend immediately. However, ensure that the player recovers the defending distance of one metre (three feet), since this will undoubtedly have been shortened during her efforts to win the ball.

BUILDING PRACTICES

All too often a new coach simply wants to build up a reservoir of practices. Initially, the answer can be to use other people's ideas, but ultimately any coach needs to generate ideas for herself.

There are several sources available to the coach for obtaining the necessary ideas:

O reference books with practices detailed, as in a later section of this chapter (see page 33)
O handouts from coaching courses
O results of playing with practices

In organising practice sessions, whether using one's own ideas or those from other coaches, certain rules should be obeyed.

O know the aim of the practice
O get as many players active as possible, giving maximum opportunity for practice
O ensure that you are in a position, when coaching, to see all players working
O voice should be pitched low, particularly if the coach has to speak loudly
O give coaching points for all stages, but not all at once
O if the practice does not produce what is required, then exchange it for another that has the same aim
O get the result of the original aim before identifying and asking for the next: *be single-minded*

It should be that the aims start simply, like the practices. As progress is made, so the aim of the practice is more difficult to obtain. This is why the aims as well as the practices need to have structure and levels of achievement.

Sample practices

The sample practices given in the next section have their aim defined, and have been set out in a progressive sequence. It is quite possible that only one or two of the practices will be coped with during a session. If a modification to them is made, ensure that the aim still remains: do not confuse your players.

Playing with practices

A beginner or an experienced player can and should play with practice ideas. There are several ways of doing this:

O with pen and paper, setting them out in a similar way to the sample practices described in the next section
O with a set of magnets and a magnetic board
O with a group of players

For the purpose of 'playing practices', take a group of three and position them in a triangular formation. This forms the basis of all the following examples (see Figure 10 for basic diagram, and page vii for key to symbols used).

Fig. 10

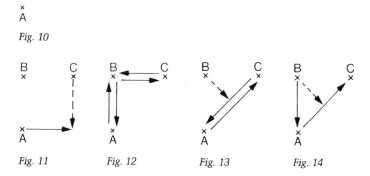

Fig. 11   *Fig. 12*   *Fig. 13*   *Fig. 14*

Example 1

Aim: to introduce pivot and make the player aware of feet when ready to pass

A has ball. C runs to space, to receive ball. C turns using pivot to face empty space, and passes ball to B who moves into it (Figure 11).

Example 2

Aim: to improve ball familiarisation

Set closer together.
A drops ball to B, who pushes it to C. C lifts it high back to B, who jumps to push it back to A (Figure 12).
Change position of players after three sequences.

Example 3

Aim: to improve the timing for getting free

A and C are passing the ball back and forth rhythmically. B gets ready to sprint and, when she feels that the ball can be taken out of the air, she runs forward to do so (Figure 13). If successful, return ball to A; repeat exercise again.

Example 4

Aim: to improve interception technique at the receiving end

B passes to A, and immediately after releasing the ball runs to intercept the pass from A to C. If successful, return ball to A; C returns to original point (Figure 14). Start sequence again.

The examples given above indicate how one particular practice pattern can be used and developed for a variety of aims.

The practice should not be complicated and, with a ratio of working one to resting two, will give the coach time to assess the working player.

Results

The coach should be aware that achieving a practice aim is pleasing to both coach and player alike. It is by acknowledging the attainment of an aim, and continually pushing playing performance, that the appetite to progress forward will be maintained.

SKILLS PRACTICES

Footwork

Aim 1: to obtain a one/two landing on the correct foot, in a balanced position ready to throw

Sample practice

i   On own, running around court, jumping to land on a line on coach's whistle.
ii 2s (Figure 15). A runs to take ball from B, which is thrown above head height.
iii 2s; 1 static; 1 working (Figure 16). A runs to side to take pass from B; pass to be put up and out to the side. A then corrects footwork before returning ball to B. A then runs but to the left side, and so on.

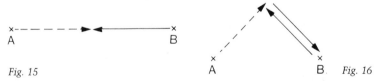

Fig. 15   A   B. Fig. 16

Observations (see page 14)

O stride pattern
O elevation
O top of body upright
O which is correct foot down first
O placement of second foot
O weight back
O full contact between landing foot and the ground

Aim 2: to introduce the pivot and make the player aware of feet positioning

Sample practice

i   Start with *iii* above. After landing ask for pivot before returning ball to B. Both feet should be pointing at B before a return throw is attempted (Figure 17).

ii   4s (Figure 17). A runs to take pass from D; lands, then pivots and returns ball to D. Continues running to point Y. B then does the same, and so on.

iii   A throws to D, who has run forward to meet the pass. D pivots, and returns ball to C. D continues running and goes behind B. C then throws to A who has run forward. A pivots, returns ball to B. A continues running to go behind C, and so on (Figure 18).

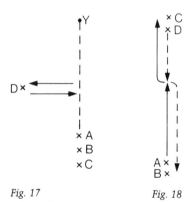

Fig. 17   Fig. 18

Observations (see page 16)

O   landing foot is pivot foot
O   pivot on ball of foot
O   short pushes
O   shortest way to receiver
O   both feet pointing at receiver

Catching

Aim 3: to improve ball familiarisation

Sample practice

i   On own with ball, throwing it from side to side, making arc wider and wider (Figure 19).

ii   Winding the ball around neck, then waist, then hips, and finally ankles. Pass the ball from hand to hand around the body. N.B. Remember to practise passing the ball in either direction.

iii 2s – 1 ball (Figure 20a). A throws to B who returns to A. Work on right hand of A and left of B; then reverse process.

iv 2s – 2 balls (Figure 20b). Keep two balls going, same practice as *iii*.

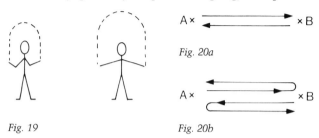

Fig. 20a

Fig. 19   Fig. 20b

Observations (see page 17)

- O shape of hand
- O sign of tension
- O giving of wrist and arm
- O no 'smacking' heard
- O competent both hands
- O all levels and wings tested

Aim 4: to improve two-handed catching technique

Sample practice

i On own with ball, throw into air, and snatch to holding position. Drop and snatch; throw over shoulder, turn and pull to body.

ii 2s – 1 ball. A faces B approximately 1m (3ft) apart. 1 working, 1 static. Put ball high to worker, take out of air, land balanced and controlled, then pass ball back. Gradually extend distance, making pass more difficult to take with two hands.

iii 2s – 1 ball (Figure 21). B passes to A, then runs to the right to take high return pass from A. B then returns ball to A who drops it short for B to run and collect it. B then returns ball to A, then runs to the left to take a high pass from A – and so on.

Observations (see page 17)

- O elevation and stretch for high ball
- O fingers open, two hands used
- O hands at the sides of ball, thumbs behind
- O watching ball into hands
- O catch to 'holding' position
- O feet are balanced on landing (see page 16)
- O take ball early where possible

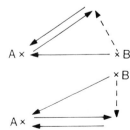

Fig. 21

Throwing

Aim 5: to improve footwork with regard to passing technique

Sample practice

i   Start with the practice listed in *Aim 2i*. Vary distance between A and B so that both long and short distance passes are made.

ii In 3s (Figure 22). Work C for about six passes before changing over. Insist that feet and weight are correctly positioned *before* the throw is made. When practising, vary distance of C from A and B, to effect different passing types. For long distance, encourage use of shoulder pass; for shorter distance, a two-handed pass.

Observations (see page 18)

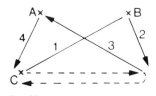

Fig. 22

O   landing foot is correct
O   weight over landing foot
O   transference of weight
O   landing foot is not being dragged
O   position of 'looking foot'

Aim 6: to improve execution speed of a throw, starting from the 'holding' position

Sample practice

i   On own with ball and wall. Mark spot on wall. Practise one-handed (right or left) and two-handed passes, taking ball from central position, through preparation, release and follow-through stages.

ii In 4s. C throws ball to herself and catches it centrally; a pass is then made to either A or B. D is the defender who attempts to read information concerning the pass given by C. Start C close to A and B, giving D very little time to react. Gradually move C back.

Observations (see page 18)

O   catch to 'holding' position
O   feet correct with weight over landing foot
O   minimum pause time, holding to release
O   weight transference
O   arm and finger extension
O   follow through in direction of pass

Aim 7: to improve the 'when to throw'

Sample practice

i   In 2s. Mark a point on the floor, or use a line. A has ball; when B reaches line she receives pass. Make this more precise by asking B to move at speed to this mark. The pass from A should reach B as she reaches the mark.

ii   In 4s. A and B pass the ball slowly and deliberately between themselves. C keeps defender D on the move. C can move to line Y or Z, and when this final movement is seen by A or B the ball should be passed to C.

Observations (see page 19)

O   landing balanced and controlled
O   landing facing attacking play
O   catching action central
O   transference of weight
O   receiver has made final movement to get free

Aim 8: to improve the 'where' to put the ball

Sample practice

i   In 2s (Figure 23). A walks slowly to right with hand out ahead at a desired height. B makes pass, hitting hand of A. A returns ball to B, and then walks to left. Extend this practice by increasing speed of A, eventually allowing A to catch ball with two hands. Further extension to this should be carried out, allowing A angled movement toward or away from B.

Observations (see page 19)

O   thrower having upright body position
O   feet correct with weight over landing foot
O   hands on ball, one or two
O   weight transference
O   arm and finger extension
O   follow through in direction of pass
O   body position on release
O   indication by receiver
O   space for 'where'
O   height of pass

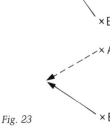

Fig. 23

Aim 9: to improve the technique of getting free, using a sprint

Sample practice

i   On own between two selected lines (Figure 24). Coach selects line to
    sprint to. On whistle, sprint to selected line. Resume middle position.
ii In 2s, practise as above (Figure 25). A selects line to sprint to. B stays
    with her. Coach blows whistle for A to sprint to appropriate line.
iii In 3s (Figure 26). C has ball. B marks A. C throws ball to herself and
    within three seconds passes ball to A, who has made her sprint to get
    free. Ensure A uses both right and left sides to sprint to.

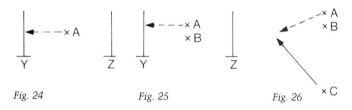

Fig. 24   Fig. 25   Fig. 26

Observations (see page 25)

O   weight evenly distributed
O   knees flexed
O   narrow footbase
O   feet and body turn with slight overbalance
O   short punchy strides into ground
O   short distance, speed maintained
O   body is not bent over

*Aim 10: to improve the technique of getting free, using a
change of direction*

Sample practice

i   On own – A in the middle of two lines. Move to left to line Y; change
    direction and sprint to line Z.
ii Put in opponent B as i above. Allow A to select any point up to line Y
    to effect the change of direction and sprint to line Z. Coach should
    ensure that B shadows A and does not hold back from marking her thus
    making the change of direction inappropriate.
iii As for ii, but put in thrower C, so that when return movement is made
    A is made to catch pass at line Z.

These change-of-direction practices work on the horizontal plane,
although it need not necessarily be so. The coach should not, however,
encourage changes of direction such that the receiver is running away from
the ball, unless the players' throwing skills can cope.

Observations (see page 25)

- ○ weight evenly distributed
- ○ knees flexed
- ○ narrow footbase
- ○ short even strides
- ○ total body commitment to first direction
- ○ released-spring action into second direction
- ○ braking leg bent
- ○ maintenance of speed in second direction

Aim 11: to improve the timing for getting free

Sample practice

i   In 2s. A has ball. A puts ball to floor. B gets ready and reacts to A picking up ball and passing to B, who has sprinted to a space. B then puts ball down, A gets ready, and so on.

ii In 3s (Figure 27). A moves to left. C passes to A. B gets ready. When C has received return pass from A she passes to B. A returns to centre line ready to start again. Note that distance for A and B to run is short.

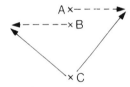

Fig. 27

Observations (see page 25)

- ○ watch player with ball
- ○ state of readiness
- ○ narrow footbase
- ○ thrower ready
- ○ total commitment with final movement
- ○ speed maintained

Aim 12: to improve the 'where' to get free

Sample practice

i   On own in space. Get ready. On coach's whistle, player sprints to another free space, and so on.

ii In 3s – 1 ball. A has ball. B sprints to a space to receive pass from A: a right angle should be attempted. C then sprints to a space to receive pass from B and so on. Do not allow receiver to run away from thrower.

iii In 3s (Figure 28a). C throws to B. A moves to space to receive ball from B. A has freedom to move to any of the marked spaces. A then returns ball to C and resumes central position before starting again.

iv In 4s (Figure 28b). B marks A. D passes to C. A gets free into space to take ball from C. B should continually move around A so that the open moving space is not so obvious for A to determine.

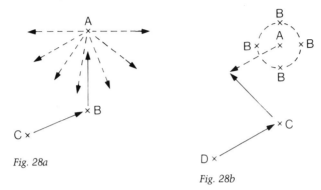

Fig. 28a

Fig. 28b

Observations (see page 25)

O receiver not standing in receiving space
O state of readiness
O defender unable to get there first
O speed, if used, to be maintained
O running away from ball
O aware of player with ball
O aware of any other defender

A ×

B ×

Defending

Aim 13: to introduce stage 1 man-to-man marking, concentrating on shadowing of opponent

C ×

Sample practice

Fig. 29

i   In 2s. B shadowing A. A moves slowly side to side, B to stay close to her.
ii In 2s. B shadowing A. Free movement for A around court, B to stay close. On whistle, B should be able to touch A.
iii In 3s. C has ball (Figure 29). A moves from side to side for a count of three seconds, then she must get free immediately for pass from C. B attempts to keep A covered so that the ball cannot reach A.

Observations (see page 26)

○ close to opponent but not touching
○ can see opponent
○ state of readiness
○ narrow footbase for quick movement in either direction
○ able to stay with opponent for three or more seconds
○ total commitment with final movement

Aim 14: to improve the interception of the pass at the receiving end

Sample practice

i   In 2s (Figure 30). A starts behind a line. B passes to A, who has to take the ball to the side and in front of the line.
ii In 4s (Figure 31). A keeps on the move. B must stay with her for a count of more than three seconds. C counts and on count of four passes to D. B attempts to intercept this pass.

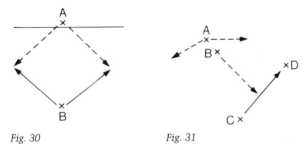

Fig. 30   Fig. 31

Observations (see page 27)

○ standing off opponent slightly
○ can see opponent
○ state of readiness
○ narrow footbase for quick movement in either direction
○ angled interception where possible
○ stride lengthened on interception
○ body pulled away on interception
○ final commitment is *total*

Shooting

Aim 15: to improve the technique of the standing shot

Sample practice

On own in circle, taking shots from different positions in circle. Vary flight of ball to goal.

ii   In 2s (Figure 32). B stands outside circle – A passes to her. B corrects footwork, shoots and rebounds, returning ball to A and going to opposite side. Continue for approximately ten sequences.

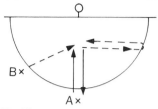

Fig. 32

Observations (see page 28)

O   landing foot is front foot
O   other foot placed comfortably behind
O   weight over back foot, knee bent
O   ball at high position on flat of hand
O   release point remains high
O   back of ring is aimed for
O   follow through of arm and fingers

Throw-up

Aim 16: to improve the technique of the throw-up

Sample practice

i   In 2s – A throwing ball into air, B snatching it away.
ii   In 4s. Set up a throw-up situation.
iii C is the umpire putting the ball into space for either A or B to win (Figure 33). D is waiting and, depending on who wins the ball, goes to receive a pass. Whoever loses throw-up attempts to defend the pass immediately.

Observations (see page 29)

O   open body to umpire
O   hands relaxed at sides
O   knees flexed, with back vertical and straight
O   watch ball
O   snatch away, turning the body to protect
O   pause before passing

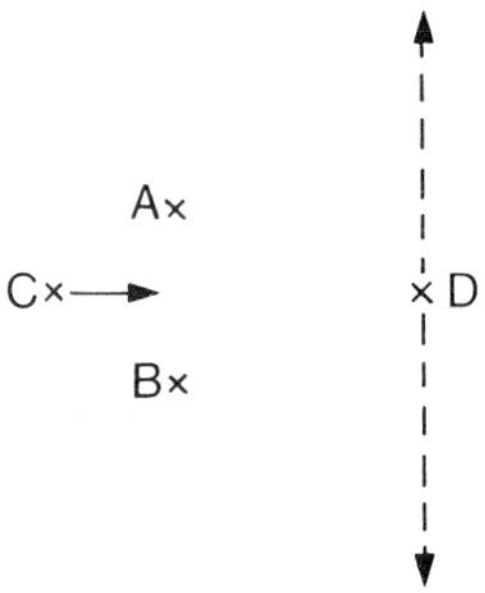

Ax

Cx⟶   ×D

Bx

Fig. 33

Chapter 3

Developing the basic skills of netball

Heather Crouch

Heather Crouch, M.Ed., *is a senior lecturer at Anglia Polytechnic. She was the England Coach from 1983 to 1987, the England Manager for the 1983 World Tournament in Singapore, an England selector for ten years, and the England Under 21 and Under 18 Coach. She is a life member and vice president of Essex Metropolitan County Netball Association.*

This chapter starts from the assumption that the players are reasonably competent in the basic skills. They can throw and catch the netball, they understand and can adhere to the footwork rules, their shooting is reasonable, they are fairly proficient at getting free, and they can mark an opponent. They know enough about the rules of netball and the responsibilities of each playing position on court to play an adequate game of netball.

Many coaches would be delighted to reach this 'adequate' stage with their squad of players. However, it is hoped that most coaches thirst for new ideas and ways to progress and develop the skill levels of their players. Enthusiasm and enjoyment are the results of offering stimulating challenges to players so that their range of ability and understanding is continually expanded.

The enhanced tactical play of a team is commensurate to the level of skill of the individual players. For example, a team is unlikely to succeed in playing a fast attack if players have not acquired the skill of turning in the air to land facing their own goal.

It is difficult to decide whether the tactical plan is determined first and then the necessary skills developed, or whether as the skills progress new tactical ideas emerge. In reality, probably both occur. Coaches concerned with 'developing the skills' should not just focus upon increasing the repertoire of skills of individuals so that players can 'perform' practices faultlessly. Players must be placed in increasingly pressurised situations where they, not always the coach, have to make decisions as to what is the appropriate skill, and *when* to execute that skill.

The distinction between skill and tactical development is unavoidably hazy. All too frequently coaches concern themselves with trying to dream up new practices or, worse still, work through a practice devised by someone else without adapting and developing it to suit their own particular players. The initial aim ought to be to observe and evaluate the shortcomings of team performance in order to identify which skill(s) needs improving, then devise, or select, game-like practice situations which allow that skill to be learnt, practised and developed.

This process of identification is not easy since, the more the skills of netball are developed, the more there seems to be a tendency for originally distinct skills to merge together. For example, intercepting the ball can look like, and indeed can be coached as, the skill of catching the ball. Similarly, the attacking skill of protecting space is almost identical to blocking, the defending skill which prevents the opponent from moving into advantageous space. Most obviously, the primary basic skills of footwork, throwing and catching usually occur as one continuous flowing action when performed by more skilful players.

The interdependence between tactical ideas and necessary skill level is further discussed in Chapter 4. It is sufficient here to realise that, the greater the range of skills, so an increasing number of tactical ideas become possible, while at the same time new tactics can highlight the need for improved skill levels.

ADDING VARIETY TO THE BASIC SKILLS

Netballers must be encouraged to add variety and develop variations to the basic skills so that match play does not become a stereotyped performance by predictable players. Even a continuously winning team should be concerned with developing the skill level of the individual players, so that alternative actions can be made when the situation demands. For example, players who always catch the ball in two hands, land with first one foot, then the other, pivot and then pass (perhaps predictably with a two-handed pass) will be much easier to defend than the player who can, if necessary, catch the ball, turn in the air (either clockwise or anticlockwise) and release the ball with either hand before landing. Arguably the entertainment value of our game is also enhanced once versatile, flairful players take to the court.

This chapter is intended to encourage coaches to be observant and identify which aspects of the players' skill(s) warrant further development. Figure 34 is a synopsis of possible variations and developments to the basic skills of netball, and the remainder of the chapter focuses on some of the subsequent aims which emerge.

Coaches need to decide when, or if, such aims might be relevant to their group of players. Observations and coaching points are made in order to help with that decision making. Any practice situations are merely ideas which have worked for me and my players. Other coaches may wish to try them only as a stimulus to create and develop their own practices which are relevant to their own players. Practice situations should always be in a state of flux, with alterations being made according to the changing levels of skill and understanding of the players, and to changing team strategies.

FOOTWORK

Footwork underlines all the other skills of netball. The position of the

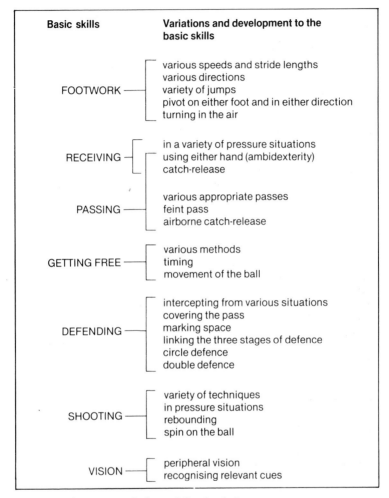

Basic skills	Variations and development to the basic skills
FOOTWORK	various speeds and stride lengths various directions variety of jumps pivot on either foot and in either direction turning in the air
RECEIVING	in a variety of pressure situations using either hand (ambidexterity) catch-release
PASSING	various appropriate passes feint pass airborne catch-release
GETTING FREE	various methods timing movement of the ball
DEFENDING	intercepting from various situations covering the pass marking space linking the three stages of defence circle defence double defence
SHOOTING	variety of techniques in pressure situations rebounding spin on the ball
VISION	peripheral vision recognising relevant cues

Fig. 34 Developments to the basic skills of netball

body for throwing and catching, the ability to stop, change direction and get away from an opponent, the various defensive stances and the variety of shooting techniques are all dependent on sound yet versatile footwork.

Aim: to develop various running speeds and stride lengths

Netball involves stopping, starting, and changing direction to travel backwards, sideways and diagonally as well as forwards, so coaches should remember to offer opportunities for players to practise this range of footwork patterns. The warm-up period before training or 'skills drills' for fitness work could include such activities as player A sprinting from 0 to 1, then running backwards to 0, then sprinting to 2 and so on (Figure 35). Jumps can soon be added so that, for example, the jump at the circle edge is a high wide leap, while the jump at the goalpost, 0, is a sargeant jump, off two feet. The step patterns can be altered to, say, side-steps and the types of jumps can be changed too. A ball may also be thrown at the player so that, as she reaches the circle edge, it must be caught and returned to the feed before A is forced to land 'offside' outside the circle. The permutations are numerous, and coaches should keep in mind the aim to develop versatile yet appropriate footwork when planning practices.

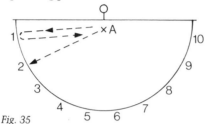

Fig. 35

Aim: to develop the ability to jump and land in a variety of ways

Coaches should not insist on players always landing on the same foot. Differing playing situations demand different step patterns (so long as the rules governing footwork are not infringed). Assuming a player jumps, catches the ball and lands then five basic step patterns are possible:

i   A two-footed take-off and a two-footed landing. Example: a GS (Goal Shooter) who wants to 'hold' firmly, then jump to receive a high pass.

ii A one-footed take-off and a two-footed landing. Example: a WA (Wing Attack) or C (Centre) as she takes off from a run to receive the ball with a 'split landing' on the attacking circle edge.

iii A two-footed take-off and a one-footed landing. Example: a GK (Goal Keeper) jumping to collect a rebound, then making a pass.

iv Taking off from one foot and landing on the same foot. Example: making an interception to the left-hand side by taking off and landing on the left foot.

v   Taking off from one foot and landing on the other. Example: a WD (Wing Defence) receiving an easy pass, landing on the right foot, and ready then to step forward onto the left to make a long shoulder pass.

Once the player has landed on one or both feet, the rules governing footwork permit various other moves which involve the lifting of the landing foot so long as it is not then grounded before the ball is released. Examples include landing on two feet, stepping forward onto one in order to jump high and release the ball while airborne or, having landed on one foot, settling with both feet grounded and then jumping high off two feet (to clear a defence) and, again, passing while airborne. Remember also that two-footed landings may need to be compact (if falling offside) or widely spread, and also that the legs can be 'split' in a sideways or forwards/backwards direction.

A jump pass to clear the defence

Split landing as GS receives the ball

GS holding firm to receive
high overhead pass

The 'forward/back' split leg action of
the GS

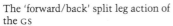

WA using split landing
on the edge of the
attacking circle

Aim: to develop the ability to use a pivot

Different playing situations demand that players should be able to pivot effortlessly in either direction and on either foot, whether it is the landing or non-landing foot. This ability is required most obviously after receiving the ball, but also as a means of getting away from a defence or as a means of linking different stages of defending skills.

Examples

i   The 'long' pivot can be used by a WA who has only just beaten a fast WD to the ball on a centre pass (Figure 36). The WA might wish deliberately to turn her back to the WD in order to protect the ball, which may also result in her subsequent pass – to a GA or GS being relatively undefended.

ii   Alternatively, if the WD does not break away so swiftly, it may be better for the WA to pivot the 'short' way round so that her GA and C stay in her sights and the ball can be passed to them more quickly (Figure 37).

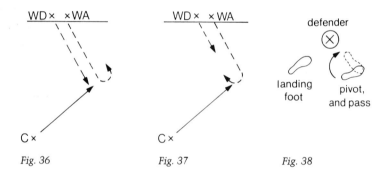

Fig. 36   Fig. 37   Fig. 38

iii The pivot can be used also to help 'get round' a defence who is covering the ball (Figure 38). Instead of pivoting on the landing foot, the player with the ball steps forward to the side of the defence, then pivots on the non-landing foot away from the defence before releasing the ball.

iv   Clever use of the pivot can help a GS or GA gain space towards the goalpost. The shooter holds the ball high and looks to shoot, so the defence must move 90cm (3ft) away. The GS then steps forward onto her non-landing foot (to take up the 90cm distance), pivots on that foot and lays the ball out to the C or WA who are hugging the circle edge, before regrounding her landing foot. The C or WA returns the ball immediately. The GS may receive the ball while grounded or jump and land 1, 2 or ideally jump and use a split landing, thus gaining about two metres (6½ft) towards the goalpost.

v   The 'reverse pivot' may be used to aid attacking or defending moves. For example, at a centre pass a WA being pressurised by a fast WD can step forward (in this example, onto her right foot) into the centre third only to reverse pivot (on her right foot) back behind the WD and then receive the pass (Figure 39). This type of pivot action is effective only if the WD is convinced that the WA intends to burst straight out into the centre third.

The reverse pivot at centre pass

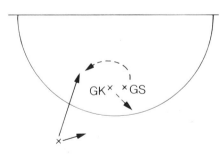

Fig. 39   *Fig. 40*

The same move can be useful to a GS who, in this example (Figure 40), indicates she wants the ball to be passed across the front of the circle, and succeeds in tempting the GK to edge between her and the feed. As soon as the GK begins to commit herself forward, the GS reverse pivots behind the GK and then receives the ball. In both instances the pivot occurs on the foot nearest to the feed and the player who is pivoting must turn her back to her opponent. Timing is crucial: as the defender commits herself forward, the reverse pivot behind the defence is executed.

vi The usefulness of the reverse pivot in defending is looked at in the section on defence.

Aim: to develop a turn in the air when catching the ball, either to maintain a fast attack, or to act as protection against the defence. The turn in the air obviates the pivot. It is initiated at take-off by the placement of the feet, but most particularly by the action of the hips, which thrust round in the direction of the turn. There will be more turning time the higher the player jumps.

Practice situations

Any 'catch, land, pivot, pass' practices can be used, but the emphasis becomes 'catch, turn, and pass'. For example:

i As A (Figure 41) runs forward to receive the ball from B, the ball should be sent to either the left or the right of A. Assuming the ball is sent to her right, A should turn with the ball; i.e., in a clockwise direction. When the ball is thrown to the left side of the receiver, it should be caught in the left hand and the impetus of the ball used to assist the player to turn in an anticlockwise direction (Figure 42). A passes the ball to C, then runs behind D. C now passes to B as she runs forward, and the practice becomes continuous.

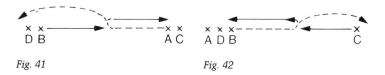

Fig. 41   *Fig. 42*

By throwing the ball deliberately to either side of the on-coming player, the thrower is the person determining which way the receiver should turn. If a defence is added to play against the on-coming player the situation becomes more realistic, with the thrower being expected to recognise the receiver's 'free' side. When the ball is thrown directly at the on-coming player, the receiver has to make the decision as to which way to turn. In other words, the thrower should become aware that she can help a tightly defended team-mate.

The practice can progress so that, as A is turning in the air ready to send the ball to C, C moves suddenly left or right and A has to respond appropriately (Figure 43).

ii In most attacking moves, the player receiving the ball will not be expected to turn the ball through 180°. A 90° turn of the ball may be more common.

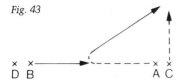

Fig. 43

Three players are set up on three corners of a square. C runs straight and receives a pass from A at the empty corner (Figure 44a). (Hopefully this set-up will have been learnt earlier when practising the pivot.) The receiver catches the ball while airborne and turns the 'short' way round (i.e., 90°, by turning in towards the middle of the square). The practice continues with C passing to B, so that B can catch, turn in the air and land to face the new empty corner (Figure 44b). Correct timing of the run onto the ball needs to be maintained.

Players may need to be able to turn the long way round with the ball – i.e., away from the defending player – and the practice can be easily adapted (Figure 45). A particular area for coaches to give

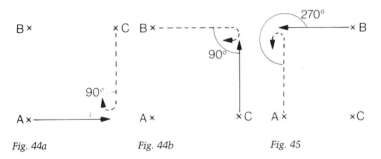

Fig. 44a   *Fig. 44b*   *Fig. 45*

attention to is the rebalancing of the player after the turn and the landing, before the throw is made. A common fault is for the body weight to be falling backwards during the throw. Feet must be adjusted so that the body weight is transferred forward into the subsequent pass.

Other adaptations include

O one- or two-handed airborne passes while turning
O catch-release while turning

RECEIVING

Players may become proficient at catching the ball safely with two hands in 'easy' situations. However, coaches need to identify those conditions under which players drop or mishandle the ball. Game-like situations then need to be set up which allow players to practise so that the ball can be safely caught or redirected in a controlled manner, even when conditions mitigate against easy catching. Examples of such 'pressurised' conditions include instances when a player is

O   jumping high: (a) from a 'static' position and possibly being knocked by the opposition; (b) from running onto the ball, and including intercepting the ball
O   retrieving the ball from 'a rebound'
O   tipping the ball while at maximum stretch, then catching it
O   catching the ball with one hand (either hand)
O   controlling the ball as it and/or the player go offside
O   volleying the ball
O   retrieving the loose ball
O   being tightly defended
O   being double-marked
O   running forward onto the ball
O   receiving the ball at right angles (see Chapter 2)
O   receiving various passes; e.g., bounce
O   standing still
O   receiving the ball from relatively 'blind' situations

This list is not exhaustive, but the identification of such situations should inform the creation (or selection) of relevant skills practices. Some situations may relate to particular playing positions (circle players for rebounds, a GS for receiving a high pass from a static position) but most are catching or retrieving situations which all team members should be given an opportunity to practise.

Aim: to improve ball handling, but specifically the ability to catch the ball

Catching the ball from a 'blind' situation puts the receiver in a type of pressurised situation, since the normal information (or cues) relating to the speed and direction of the pass is not received until the last moment.

Practice situation

i   B stands with her back to A and about 1.8 – 2.4m (6 – 8ft) distant. A holds the ball, calls 'right' and passes the ball to the right of B, who immediately pivots round to the right to receive the ball. The pass should be sufficiently sympathetic and well timed for B to be able to catch the ball. Calls of 'left', 'high', 'low', etc., can also be made with the resultant appropriate feed.

ii A pressure situation can be set up by using two netballs and three players in a triangular formation (Figure 46). A is under pressure, so that B passes a ball to A who passes it back to B, then immediately C passes the second ball to A, who returns it to C. B and C work to see how fast they can feed A without her dropping the ball. The types of passes can be varied (e.g., bounce, chest, under), so everyone has to think about what is required. The practice can progress with B and C

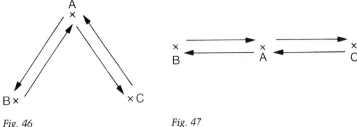

Fig. 46   *Fig. 47*

moving further around A until the triangular formation becomes a straight line, so that, once again, A is receiving the ball from a relatively 'blind' situation (Figure 47).

iii Another progression is to add two more players, so that A is in the middle of a square formed by B, C, D and E. B feeds the ball to A, who then lays the ball off to E. C immediately feeds the second ball to A, who then lays it off to D. By then B should be ready to pass the first ball again (Figure 48). The type of passes, their height, strength and direction, can be dictated by the coach, or randomly selected by the players.

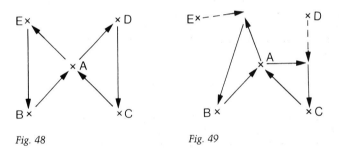

Fig. 48   *Fig. 49*

A progression involves D moving just as A receives the ball from C, so that A has to react and send the ball ahead of the moving player. Similarly E could move, and indicate for the ball as A receives the pass from B. This can be tiring work for D and E (Figure 49).

Yet another progression involves all five players maintaining their formation as they move down the length of the court (obeying the footwork rules). This also helps to develop peripheral vision.

Aim: to develop ambidexterity in order to make players more versatile and adaptive. Ambidexterity is needed not just for catching and passing but also for intercepting and defending the pass or shot, and for rebounding. Practices to encourage players to use either hand should be introduced as early as possible. Even beginners can cope with the ball familiarisation practices identified in Chapter 2.

Practice situations

(a) *Catching* with either hand is likely to be a skill required by most players, since at maximum stretch a player can reach further with one hand than with two.

i   When a player is stretching to her right she should receive the pass in her right hand while landing on her right foot (Figure 50a). Similarly, a ball thrown to the left should be received in the left hand, with the player landing on her left foot (Figure 50b).

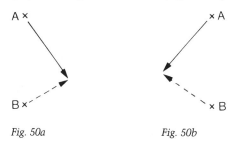

Fig. 50a   Fig. 50b

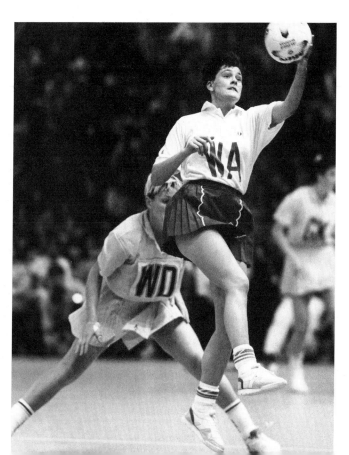

ii   In 3s passing the ball down court in a 'figure of eight' formation (Figure 51).

A, B and C stand in a line facing down the court, with B holding a ball. A runs forward and receives B's pass, which is sent ahead of A so that she stretches to receive the ball in her left hand, landing on her left foot (Figure 51a). B then runs behind A. C runs forward to receive a pass from A which is sent ahead of C so that she stretches to receive the ball in her right hand, landing on her right foot (Figure 51b). A then runs behind C and the practice continues with C passing to B (Figure 51c). Astute observation and relevant feedback are required from the coach.

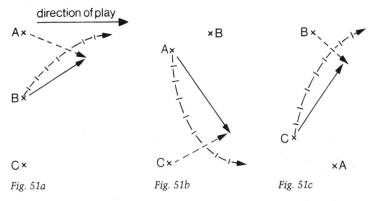

direction of play

Fig. 51a   Fig. 51b   Fig. 51c

In the first instance, this action of catching the ball in one hand may, for safety's sake, be followed by putting the second hand on as soon as possible. However, an ambidexterous catch can soon develop into a catch-release action, where the ball can be controlled with just one hand.

(b) Throwing, with either hand, can be helpful in avoiding an opponent's defending action, particularly when she 'covers' the ball. The basic points relating to foot positioning, transference of body weight and so on will need to be reiterated once a player starts to use her least dominant hand. It may be more realistic and appropriate to begin with short, lay-off passes being practised before looking at longer passes with either hand. The variety of actions to feint the pass can be increased once a player can control and pass the ball with either hand.

(c) Intercepting, defending the pass or shot and rebounding should also be attempted using either hand. Defences can help to prevent their opponents from settling down by using unpredictable and versatile defending actions. Variations include intercepting the ball with the right hand and then passing with the left or vice versa (be sure not to infringe the ball-handling rule). This may be useful for the player who can catch or intercept with either hand but who has not yet mastered ambidexterous throwing.

Aim: to develop catch-release of the ball as one continuous action in order to speed up attacking play. The aim is to convert the impetus on the ball when it is caught into the subsequent controlled throw. Initially, wherever the receiver first puts her hands (or hand) on the ball should be the point of release for the return pass. The action is not to smack the ball; fingers should be spread, wrists (particularly) and elbows should 'give' on receiving the ball. Time should not be wasted by pulling the ball into the body; instead players should think merely of redirecting the flight of the ball, not actually stopping it.

Practice situations

In 2s, with A and B facing. A feeds the ball sympathetically to B, but stretches her high, low and wide. B catch-releases the ball back to A; when the ball is sent to her right B uses her right hand only, and vice versa on the left. If the ball is sent straight at her, B uses both hands to catch-release. Progress to working in 3s, so that a change of direction of pass can occur. Start with only one or two players working on the catch-release action and build up to all three practising the skill simultaneously.

Any of a coach's 'normal' practices for catching and throwing can be adapted to include opportunities to practise the catch-release action. Further developments to the skill include the airborne catch-release, including using either hand. Attack-minded defences may enjoy practising intercept-release.

PASSING

It has already been suggested that the distinction between the skills of catching and passing becomes less obvious when performed by more skilful players. The principles of throwing (identified in Chapter 2) still apply, but the distinct preparation and follow-through phases of a beginner's pass can be reduced and transference of weight can seem to disappear. The repertoire of actions related to passing is broadened to include catch-release, airborne passing, feinting the pass, passing with either hand and using a greater variety of passes.

Aim: to develop a variety of passes, so as to make players less predictable to the opposition and able to use the appropriate pass for any given situation.

Essentially, a variety of passes will result from varying the release point of the ball (see photographs). The player who always releases the ball from two hands at chest height will be much easier to defend against than the player who is competent at releasing the ball from high above the head, hip-height, knee-height (for a drop/bounce pass) from either side of the body, or from points central to the body.

Various release points

High, airborne

High, two-handed

Chest height

Low release point

Practice situations

Continuous passing in 3s in a set order; i.e., from A to B to C to A, etc. As the pass is made, the passer calls 'same' or 'different'. The receiver's subsequent pass must therefore correspond to the call. This encourages players to look carefully at the sender and react quickly so that the pass remains *appropriate* (i.e., bounce and underarm passes should be short passes).

Learning the techniques of a variety of passes is basic work. Making decisions as to when, within the game, to use a particular pass requires further practice in decision-making and is closely linked with developing team, or tactical, strategies. Example situations include

O   bounce pass from circle edge to GS
O   long shoulder pass as a 'clear' from GK to the front court players
O   chest pass from C at centre pass
O   underarm pass in a close lay-off situation; e.g., WA to GA in the circle
O   lob pass to GS who is 'protecting' the space behind herself from the defence
O   the airborne throw retrieved from outside the court.

A cross-court practice which allows various passes to be used appropriately can involve 5 – 9 players (6 are used in Figure 52). C and D stand on one sideline facing E and F on the opposite sideline. A stands on court to the side of C and D, and B stands to the side of E and F away from A. C starts with the ball and passes it to A, who returns it to C as C runs across the court. C then passes to B, who passes to E. C takes the place of B and B runs behind F (Figure 52a).

The practice continues with E sending the ball to F, and so on. The running player must remember to pass and run for the return pass with the first feed, and pass and take the place of the second feed. Depending on the positioning of the two (constantly changing) feed players, the series of passes could be chest, underarm, shoulder, bounce. Other movements relating to feinting the pass, catch-release, airborne passing using either hand and so on can also be included (Figure 52b).

Variations can be introduced, such as the receiver on the side-line moving sharply left or right just before the ball is thrown to her, so the feed has to adjust to a moving player. Also, instead of merely taking the place of the second feed 'C', the cross-court runner can stop, face to face with C who returns a short pass to D, who then catch-releases the ball back to C (Figure 52c). The practice then continues as before, but with players remembering to pass and run on with the first feed, and pass and 'back up' with the second feed.

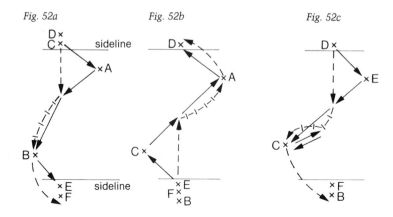

Fig. 52a   *Fig. 52b*   *Fig. 52c*

Aim: to develop the ability to feint the pass in order to avoid the ball being intercepted by the defence. The feinting action must be sufficiently convincing in order to send the opposition in one direction so that the ball may then pass, straight and direct, in another direction, out of reach of that opposition. The aim is to wrong-foot the opposition while deviating the pass as slightly as possible from its optimum pathway. A convincing feint pass involves precise, almost exaggerated movement, as if to send the ball in one direction before the ball is released in another direction. Players should be discouraged from (a) continuous ineffectual movement of the ball and (b) slight, hesitant movements that may look nothing more than nervous twitches and convince no one that a pass is intended.

Practice situations

i Three players, A, B and C, stand in a triangular formation. A prepares to throw to B; this preparation involves pushing the ball towards B (two hands on the ball), looking at B, and usually transferring body weight towards B. B has to be convinced that the ball is actually going to be sent to her, then A passes to C. C then feints the pass to A and passes to B, and so on.

As soon as a reasonable feint action has been acquired add the condition that, if A is feinting the pass to B and B does not 'respond' (i.e., A's feint was unconvincing), A should send the ball to B. In other words, if the receiver 'responds' send the ball elsewhere, if the receiver does not respond, force her to respond by sending the ball. This condition will encourage the player sending the ball to pay attention to what is going on around her. From early on the sender is being encouraged to make decisions as to when to feint the ball, not merely learning the technique of how to feint.

ii Defending players should be added as soon as possible. A feints a pass to B; if the defender, D, moves across to B the ball is sent quickly to C (Figure 53a). If D is not convinced, then the feint pass to B becomes the actual pass to B (Figure 53b). The aim is for A to realise how she can rid B or C of a defence by using a feint pass (Figure 53).

Sometimes the defence D covers the pass from A. The practice continues as before, except that now A may need to change the feint action slightly in order to step around D, or feint a high pass and actually make a bounce pass (Figure 53c).

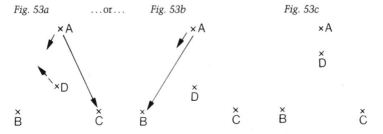

Fig. 53a ...or... *Fig. 53b* *Fig. 53c*

iii   The skill should be practised in a less static situation as soon as possible. The most convincing feint is usually one which is initially directed at another player, rather than empty space, before the ball is released. A simple, continuous practice involves four players passing to one another. The receiver must run onto the ball and the passer must move 'off' the ball. The aim is to feint the ball to one moving player but release it to another. The sequence of passing (i.e., from A to B to C to D to A, etc.) can be dictated or left undecided.

Aim: to develop airborne passing in order to speed up the attacking moves and to avoid defences covering the ball. The skill can be developed in two different ways:

O   from the player being on the ground with the ball, jumping and releasing the ball while airborne or
O   the player jumping to receive the pass and releasing the ball before landing; this may be as part of a running pass, or from a turn in the air

In both situations the coach needs to focus on the timing and coordination of the players' actions.

Since both feet are off the ground, good arm and hand actions are crucial. The throwing hand(s) needs to be behind the flight direction of the ball – i.e., a hand under the ball will result in a loopy flight path, but a hand behind the ball will result in a straight flight path (see photograph). Wrist action needs to be loose. The follow-through action should still be in the direction of the pass, although skilled players may not need to exaggerate this in the same way as beginners.

The throwing hand is *behind* the ball. This will result in the flight path of the ball being straight and direct, not loopy.

Practice situations

(a) i Players stand with a ball each, facing a wall (or netting or another player) about 2m (6½ft) away. Players jump and while airborne throw the ball at the wall. This will be easier if players have already learnt the catch-release action; otherwise the preparation to throw needs to be made before or during the jump. Players may need markers on the wall at which to aim. The practice can be made more realistic by a defence, B, covering the pass to the wall. A should jump, lifting the ball high and releasing it over B (Figure 54). Once the ball rebounds from the wall, both A and B fight to retrieve it and the practice resumes with the player without the ball as defence.

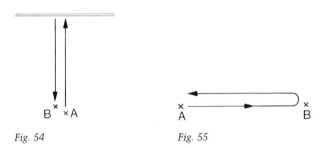

Fig. 54   *Fig. 55*

(b) i In 2s, facing, about 2m (6½ft) apart. A feeds the ball high but sympathetically to B, who has to jump to catch it. The ball is returned to A before B lands (Figure 55). Once again, if the catch-release action has been mastered then this skill of airborne passing will be easier to perform. Players should be given opportunities to practise one- and two-handed passes, and from a variety of release points (high, low, wide, etc.) Ensure that the flight of the ball is kept flat. Soon A and B ought to be able to catch-release alternatively and while airborne, thus giving a 'see-saw' effect to the practice.

ii The skill now needs to be practised in a more realistic situation. Also, those receiving a pass from a catch-release action must be made aware of the change in timing – the ball will be passed much sooner. A and B set up the see-saw practice; i.e., alternately catch-release to one another. C and D stand just behind A and B. C and D have to make sudden and correctly timed moves to their left or right in order that D can receive catch-releases from A, and C can receive catch-releases from B (Figure 56a). C and D need carefully to watch the player who will be sending them the ball. Usually they need to start their move to the left or right before the ball reaches their respective sender. C and D may need to be encouraged to indicate clearly, or to call out, so as to help the sender 'recognise' that the pass is possible. C and D can progress to sending the ball back with a catch-release action rather than merely catching the ball, then passing it back (Figure 56b).

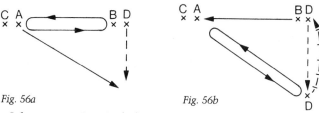

Fig. 56a   Fig. 56b

Other progressions include:

O not allowing A and B to make more than three passes before C and
   D call for the ball
O the player trying to catch-release the ball may need to practise
   sending the ball to a player who moves from a blind position. C
   makes her move and call in response to A, and D responds to B, so
   that as the ball is being sent to A, C moves sharply left or right,
   calling for the ball which is sent by A using a catch-release action. C
   would then try to catch-release the ball to B and the practice would
   continue with B responding to calls and moves from D (Figure 57)

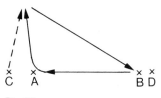

Fig. 57

iii Practice situations can also include the progression of feinting the pass,
and releasing the ball while airborne.

GETTING FREE

The purpose of 'getting free' is to create space into which the ball may be
thrown so that it can be received without being intercepted, or deflected in
any way, by the opposing team. All sorts of information will impinge on the
attack to influence her decision-making with regard to selecting the most
appropriate method of creating space. Of particular influence will be the
action of the defence, so coaches should encourage players to assess carefully
the strengths and weaknesses of their individual opponents as well as the
defending team's strategies.

Getting free from defending players can be achieved in various ways, and
the use of a sprint or sudden change of direction has been discussed in Chapter
2. Considerations of when and where to move are what add variety to this
skill.

Versatility is required, so that players have a repertoire of movements
which may be used to combat the range of defending skills of opponents. For

example, if a WA only ever sprints out fast into the centre third for the centre pass, she could be totally outplayed by any WD who could sprint faster. A sprint and stop, a sprint and dropback, or a feint and reverse pivot are three obvious alternatives.

Coaches should therefore offer opportunities for players to practise various ways of creating space, depending on the stance of the defence. When devising practice situations, coaches should remember that the player who is working on getting free should be aware of running onto the flight of the ball. Once the angle between the flight of the ball and the pathway of the receiver is less than 90° it is easier for the defence to intercept, since usually the ball passes across or over the defence (Figure 58).

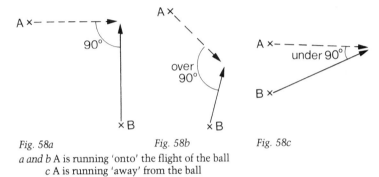

| Fig. 58a | Fig. 58b | Fig. 58c |

a and *b* A is running 'onto' the flight of the ball
c A is running 'away' from the ball

Aim: to develop various ways of getting free

The most appropriate method of getting free will depend on the stance and skill of the defence, as well as where the receiver wishes to be when the ball is caught.

i   The defence, D, may stand with her right shoulder level with the sternum (breast bone) of the attacker, A. A could (a) use a sudden

The WA has tried to get free, but her intentions have been well read by the WD

sprint to the 'open' side, hoping to out-sprint D; (b) use a sudden sprint behind D, hoping D would lose sight of her for a moment while D had to turn her head to face the new direction of A's run; (c) feint right and run behind D to the left; or (d) feint behind D and run out to the right (Figure 59 for the four alternatives).

ii   If A finds that D prefers to adopt a position behind A, then the easiest way to get free may be to run straight forward to the ball. This may be D's ploy if the forward run to the ball results in A running away from the attacking goal (Figure 60).

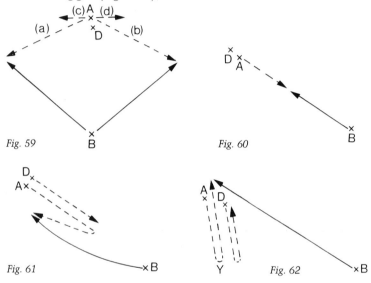

Fig. 59

Fig. 60

Fig. 61

Fig. 62

iii   If A finds that D runs forward with her, a sudden drop-back, with a high, possibly loopy pass from B, might be the most effective way (Figure 61).

   This can be developed so that A is not running away from the ball. A runs to receive the ball at Y (Figure 62). If she outsprints D then B sends her the ball. If D reaches Y at the same time, then A suddenly stops and sprints back to the starting point and B throws her the ball. The sudden change of direction can be brought about by means of pivot; experiment with the direction of the pivot as well as the most appropriate foot (usually the lead-leg, and a 'short' pivot).

iv   In selecting the most appropriate method to create space, players must also understand the team strategies, which will determine where the optimum space is for receiving the ball. (See Chapter 4 regarding basic court linkage.) If a player knows precisely where she wants to receive the ball, she may need actively to protect that space; she must work to keep space free. A will usually need to face D to prevent her from getting into the protected space (see photograph). This 'holding' action

requires quick determined side-steps, so that A is constantly between D and the space into which B needs to throw the ball. Having shielded D from the space, B throws the ball into that space, and then A pivots and runs onto the ball (Figure 63).

v   There are many situations in the game where the protective action of A may be to 'screen' a space for a team-mate, C. The skill can be practised by setting up the following situation (Figure 64): A and C

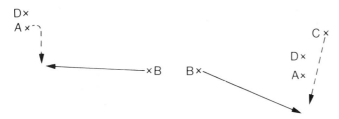

Fig. 63   Fig. 64

stand slightly apart facing B; D defends A and C as she likes. B tosses
the ball to herself and A marks D out of a space into which C runs to
receive the ball from B. This can be progressed so that, as B tosses
the all (to initiate the three-second timing), A and C have to
communicate to decide who is screening space for whom. This speeds
up decision-making and reaction time.

Aim: to develop players' awareness of correct timing with regard to getting free

The timing of the attacking move is dependent on when the thrower is
ready. The task of the coach is to help players identify, visually, the state of
readiness in different players in varying circumstances. Once players can
catch-release or send airborne passes the timing of subsequent moves will
need to be initiated earlier than if players can only 'catch, land, pivot, pass' or
'catch, turn, land, pass'. A practice described on page 51 can be useful. It can
be conditioned so that as A receives the ball she lands, pivots and passes.
However, when B receives the ball she turns in the air and lands ready to pass
straight away. C tries to catch, turn and release the ball while still airborne.
The turns and pivot may be the long or the short way round. The practice
continues with players being made sensitive to the inevitable differences in
timing of the subsequent runs to the ball (Figure 65).

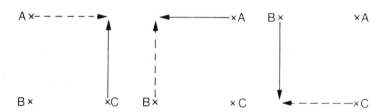

Fig. 65

Aim: to encourage players to move 'off' the ball

Having run onto the ball, it is frequently helpful for maintaining space if
players move 'off' the ball. It is difficult to say precisely where that
movement should be; usually not along the flight of the ball since this causes
crowding, but forward to some extent in order to back up team-mates.
Coaches should, therefore, be aware that the skill of passing and moving off
the ball will need to be practised. So, for example, the previous practice can
progress by adding the condition that, after every pass, the thrower must
move off the ball by running diagonally across the square; i.e., A passes to C as
she runs to the only empty corner. A moves off diagonally, immediately after
passing the ball. B now runs to the remaining empty corner and receives the
square pass from C. C then moves off diagonally and A runs to the empty
corner to receive the square pass from B, and so on (Figure 66).

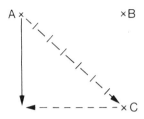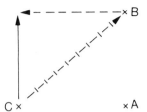

Fig. 66

All sorts of additions or variations can be made as to whether players pivot, turn, catch-release, etc. Feinting the pass can be incorporated, so that the passer feints the ball to the player running diagonally before releasing the ball for the intended square pass.

DEFENDING

Team defence strategies will be effective only if individual players have mastered specific defending skills. The basic defending skills of aiming to shadow an opponent and intercept the ball have been looked at in Chapter 2, and shall be referred to as 'stage one' defence hereafter.

Aim: to develop the ability to intercept the ball from a variety of situations

When aiming to make an interception players should be attack-orientated insofar as the intention is to repossess the ball. In order to maintain pressure on the attacking player, the defender needs continuously to adjust her position relative to her opponent. She must be able to intercept whether she comes from behind, beside or in front of her opponent, so coaches should plan practices accordingly. Players should be reminded to watch the ball, yet not lose sight of their opponent. The development of peripheral vision is an obvious requirement of a good defence.

i   *Intercepting from in front of the moving player* is covered in Chapter 2
     (aims 13 and 14). Another continuous practice which allows players to
     experience the feeling of stretching and opening out with the body,
     arms and fingers fully extended towards the ball, involves six players: a
     square formation is created with two players on the first corner, A and
     B, A holding the ball, and two players, C and D, on the second corner.
     A passes the ball square to C and immediately runs diagonally across
     the square, aiming to intercept the ball before C can pass to E. The
     practice continues with the ball being passed around the square and
     each player running off the ball diagonally, aiming to make an
     interception at the opposite corner (Figure 67).
         This practice releases the defence from having to respond to the
     movements of the attack. The commitment to intercept can be
     absolute whereas, when shadowing an opponent prior to intercepting
     the ball, short fast strides are required. Only once the ball is airborne

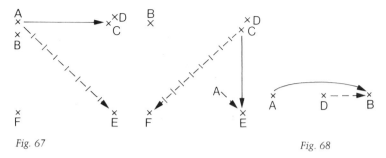

Fig. 67   Fig. 68

and it is viable for the defender to give her full attention to the ball can
her stride pattern be lengthened, culminating usually in a determined
leap towards the ball.

Frequently defences need to intercept a ball that is sent over them
to a player moving away from the ball. This can be practised by using
three players, A, B and D. A and B face each other about 9m (30ft)
apart; D stands midway between them facing A, who holds the ball. A
sends the ball over D to B. D runs back to B to intercept the ball. B
waits until D returns to the mid-point before sending the ball to A
(Figure 68).

ii   *Intercepting the ball from a static player.* No matter where the
defending player stands relative to her static opponent, the attack is
free. The free space into which the ball should be passed is diagonally
away from the defender so that, if defender D stands in front of the
attack A, the free space for A exists immediately behind herself (see
photographs). If D stands square to the left side of A, then free space is

Free space, in which to receive
the ball, is diagonally away
from the defence

Free space in which to receive
the ball

to the right of A. If D stands to the front and left of A, free space is behind and to the right of A.

However, the thrower has to recognise, precisely, where the free space is, and then 'place' the ball in absolutely the correct position. The defence should constantly readjust her position relative to potential throwers so that the attack is continuously having to reassess the free space. A defender works to offer only the least advantageous space to the attack (i.e., usually the space away from the attacking goal). She should also work to avoid getting caught 'flat' behind, or 'flat' in front of the attacker. By being sideways to the flight of the ball, it is easier to step round without causing contact, and go for the ball (see photographs). When stepping round from behind an opponent to

Defence coming from behind her opponent to intercept the ball

Defence coming round the side of her opponent to intercept the ball

intercept, footwork is important so that contact is not caused. When stepping to the right of an opponent the right foot should be placed just ahead of A and sufficiently wide so that the left foot can be brought through and placed in front of A (Figure 69). D needs to reach along the flight of the ball to meet the ball as early as possible. Similarly for intercepting or tipping a bounce pass to A, although D should bend her knees and get her body low to the ball.

Fig. 69

LF

A × Right foot

Left foot of D

Aim: to develop the ability to defend the thrower (stage two defence)

Once an opponent has received the ball (despite all attempts at interception) defenders should cover the subsequent pass. The rules of the game stipulate that the defender's feet must be at least 0.9m (3ft) from the thrower's landing foot and 'intimidation' is not permitted. This second stage of defence can have two distinct aims.

One is for the defence to stay grounded and cover the ball so that the thrower is forced to make a poor, loopy, or otherwise inaccurate pass. The intention is then that a team-mate will make the interception at the point the thrower is aiming for. The second aim can be to watch the thrower closely and jump to intercept her pass as close to the release point as possible. It is possible to try to achieve both aims, although it is difficult to spring up, or out, to intercept the ball from an initially fully stretched position. Like a spring, players need some amount of coiling up or preparation prior to the jump to intercept.

The second stage of marking is to 'cover' the thrower. This is 'grounded' stage two defence.

This Wing Defence is still defending the throw but has elected to jump

Players should be encouraged to practise switching from stage one to stage two defence as quickly as possible. Any of the previously mentioned defending practices can have stage two marking introduced into them. Be sure the 0.9m (3ft) distance is adopted before the hands are lifted to cover the ball, otherwise players will be penalised for 'obstruction'.

A 'refinement' of this skill is for the defence to cover the ball with one hand (say, the right) and keep the other hand (the left) out, covering the space forward and to the side of the ball. If the pass is to the left of the defence it should be more easily intercepted. Most attackers are, however, likely to be tempted to pass to the apparently free side of the defence. An intelligent defence will ensure that only relatively disadvantageous space is being offered. For example, a WD may 'offer' the WA the disadvantageous space along the sideline as opposed to the dominant attacking space at the crown of the circle.

Aim: to develop the ability to block the opponent out of advantageous space (stage three defence)

An advantage to the defender in staying grounded when covering the ball is that this third stage of defence can be initiated more successfully. If the defender jumps during stage two defence, then the attack can seize that opportunity to run past and continue to support her team's attacking strategies.

When blocking, the defender normally face-marks the attack and tries to keep her hips and shoulders square to the direction in which the attack wishes to run. Fast small side-steps are required to keep the defence immediately in front of the attack, and the body should be held upright. Initially this skill can be practised in 2s. A stands on one sideline of the court facing a point, Y, on the opposite sideline. D faces A, about 2m (6½ft) away, and prevents A running in a straight line to Y. D aims to force A to deviate as far away from the line AY as possible (Figure 70). In reality A would expect

Fig. 70

ultimately to reach Y, but B aims to make A's pathway to Y as long as possible, in terms of time and distance, so that, in the game situation, team offence is slowed and delayed by tight stage three marking.

Once again, this stage of defence needs to be linked to the other two stages. An earlier practice involving two attacking players, A and B, and one defence, D, can be developed to include all three stages of defence.

A tosses the ball to herself, *then* passes to B who makes a sudden sprint. D tries to intercept the ball (Figure 71a). D must not *over*commit herself

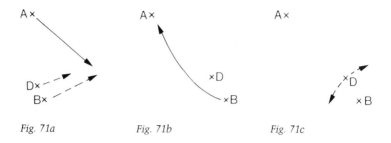

Fig. 71a   Fig. 71b   Fig. 71c

because, if B does catch the ball, D must immediately move round to cover the ball (anticipating a return pass to A) (Figure 71b). Once B passes the ball back to A, D does *not* watch the ball but attends totally to B and aims to delay B reaching A for as long as possible (Figure 71c).

Aim: to develop the ability to switch from blocking to intercepting

The next progression is for D to recognise when it is best for her to revert to focusing on the ball with an aim to interception once again (i.e., the link between stage three and stage one defence). B passes to A with D covering the pass from B. B is aiming to reach point Y and receive the return pass from A. D forces B to deviate *away* from A (Figure 72a). At the instant she feels she is beginning to turn her back to A she reverse pivots (i.e., in this instance she pivots on her left foot) round to face A, and is ready to attempt to intercept the next pass to B (Figure 72b). This final stage can now be added to the previous practice, so that B, instead of aiming merely to touch A, now works to receive the return pass from A, with D practising the change from stage three to stage one defence.

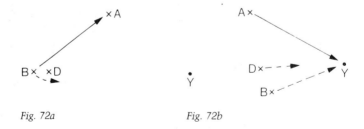

Fig. 72a   Fig. 72b

Aim: to develop the circle defence

Within the defending circle the three stages of defence appear in a modified form. The GK and GD will still be concerned with intercepting the ball, but not at the expense of leaving the goalpost and the space around it totally undefended. Stage two defence involves defending the shot at goal as well as the pass. Again, defences should aim to cover the ball with the intention of upsetting the shooting action. One hand stretches over the ball, while the other covers the space on a line between the ball and the goal. All too frequently this hand wanders ineffectually out to the side of the player. It is this higher second hand that can tip or intercept the shot as the defender jumps. Players should practise (maybe using a wall or netting) to determine their best stance for gaining the greatest reach. Hips need to be held back, over the footbase, so that the body does not topple in towards the shooter straight away. Maintaining a balanced and controlled stretch for up to three seconds, then either jumping to intercept or falling in over the ball are skills required of competent circle defences. These actions should be followed by attempts to block shooters away from the rebound. However, since the defence herself wants to retrieve the ball she must pivot to face the goal, and yet block the shooter away from the rebound by holding her ground and keeping her back continuously towards the shooter (see photographs).

GK defends the shot at goal...

then pivots round to prevent the GS gaining a possible rebound

Having retrieved the ball from the rebound, defences then need to recognise opportunities to clear the ball from the defending court and initiate the attack as quickly and safely as possible.

Communication between players is always important, but never so much as in the defending circle, when decisions to switch or to double defend need to be shared with a team-mate.

Aim: to develop the ability to double defend

If A and B mark C so that A is behind C and B in front of C, then A calls to B to move either left or right depending on C's moves, A prevents any backward movement by C and B can concentrate totally on the ball and its interception, since her sideways moves are determined by A's verbal instructions.

A and B could stand either side of C so that C can only move forward or backwards. Communication is necessary to decide which defence goes for the front ball and which for the back. This situation most frequently occurs against the GS in the circle, although in various dead-ball situations such a ploy, if unexpected, can be effective.

SHOOTING

Even after a shooter has practised so that she is scoring at least 80% of goals attempted from an undefended standing shot at goal, she still has plenty of room for improvement. In a game, the shooter is given the ball and then shoots, so she needs, if practising alone either to roll, toss or bounce the ball, to pivot or turn if necessary, and then to shoot. She should practise shooting from all points in the circle and develop the ability to score not just from a standing position but from a step-back, a step-round, a running shot, a split landing, falling off-side and so on.

If a feed is available, then a sprint, or a feint and sprint, or a 'hold' and move onto the ball can precede the shooting action. Various types of pass should be fed in, so that the shooter learns to bend her knees and get low to receive the bounce pass, or jump high without travelling to receive a high lob.

Defensive pressure also needs to be added and gradually increased, so that the shooter learns how to create and protect space into which throwers may send the ball. The ideal is to have the feed pass sent towards the goal-post. There is less room for error when the shot is taken a metre (3¼ft) from the post, rather than from, say, 4.5m (14¾ft).

Clever, controlled footwork is particularly essential in a shooter, so that she can create space to receive the ball, even against the most tenacious of defence. If the defender marks from behind, the shooter may need to spread her legs apart *sideways* in order to protect space from the defence, but at the same time she will need to stretch her arms and hands out *forward* to receive the ball (see photograph). Against the defence who stands in front of her, the shooter may need strong legs to 'hold' the defender away from the space behind. Alternatively, she may need a sprint, or feint and sprint, towards the goal-post.

Once two feeds are set up around the circle, further tactical ideas can be developed, such as when to use a reverse pivot and rotating to the post with the second shooter (Figure 73). These ideas are developed in Chapter 4.

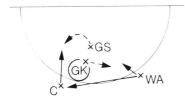

Fig. 73

Variations in step patterns will also produce a variety of shooting actions. Shooters must learn *when* to use a particular shot. For example, the running shot, or step-in (which can result in the shooting action occurring off one foot, or while airborne), is ideal when the defence has been completely left behind (see photograph below). The step-back shot may be necessary if the shooter

The result of a running shot against a defence who has been penalised

is upset by the defending action, or if the defence has been tipping previous shots at goal.

The advantages of imparting spin on the ball are discussed in Chapter 10. It may be worth noting that, if the shot is accurate enough to fall straight through the ring without touching the rim, then spin may not be a factor that needs to be considered.

VISION

A coach is not merely concerned with players being able to perform increasingly varied and complex movements. Coaches need to help players to realise *when* it is appropriate to execute a particular skill. It is the never-ending task of the coach to encourage players to observe the game and to recognise the *relevant* cues which will inform their subsequent action.

Aim: to develop peripheral vision

Players must be encouraged to widen their span of vision in order to observe more of what is going on around them. The blinkers that can exist may be removed by putting players into situations where peripheral vision and concentration are of paramount importance. For example, a circle of six or seven players should easily be able to pass a ball very quickly and accurately to one another. Just see how much more closely they have to attend to *all* players once a second ball is added to the practice. Add the condition that a ball may not be returned to the player that just threw it. Similarly, a circle of five players (four hold a ball each) can be set up round another player, A. The players forming the circle are randomly numbered, although No. 5 should be the one without a ball (Figure 74a). No. 1 calls out her number (to attract A's attention) and passes A the ball; A then passes the ball out to the only other player not holding a ball. Then No. 2 calls out her number and passes her ball to A, who then passes the ball out, again to the only 'free' player (Figure 74b). A knows she must not return the ball to the

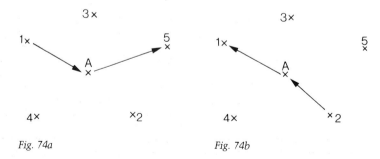

Fig. 74a   Fig. 74b

same player who made the pass. Instead she must search and/or remember where the free player is. As players become more skilful the calling can be reduced, or player A can be expected to turn in the air and land facing the free player to try to catch-release the ball.

CONCLUSION

Developing practices

In any practice, coaches should concern themselves with ensuring that players understand *why* particular skills are being developed, so that once they are playing in a match they will know *when* and *where* particular skills are appropriate. For example, a total commitment to intercept the ball may be appropriate for a WD, but not for a GD who has the added responsibility of preventing a GA from running straight to the goal. It may be appropriate for a C to receive the ball on the run if she is unmarked, but she may need a spread, split landing when running at the circle edge. So, factors such as the players' position on court, the expertise of the opposition and team strategies should serve to inform the coach with regard to the planning and development of practice situations.

Coaches need to identify which aspects of the basic skills are ready to be developed. Practices should not be progressed until a certain degree of success has been achieved; i.e., until the skill can be performed successfully about 70% of the time. The skill can be put under increasing pressure in a number of ways such as practising the skill

O   'statically'
O   on the move
O   with minimal opposition
O   with realistic opposition (or deliberately heavy opposition)
O   with alternative moves (again, opposition develops from minimum to maximum)
O   relating even more closely to the game; i.e., focusing on cues and recognising alternatives

The *rate* at which practices develop will depend on a multitude of factors, not least the ability and motivation levels of the players. These, in turn, are likely to depend on the charisma of the coach, the clarity of her organisational instructions, and the quality of the feedback she offers to players. The observational power of the coach is a crucial factor in all this.

The development of skill should be on-going. Innovation is always possible. Netball coaches in England may have much to learn from observing how the game is played in other countries. Examples include the Australian methods of dodging and their hip-height passing, the New Zealanders' zone-defending skills and the Trinidadians' airborne passing. We may also learn from other sports by observing, for example, the timing of the volleyballer's 'block', the shooting techniques of the basketball-player, the principles of the wall pass in soccer or hockey and the sprint start of the athlete.

Individual skills and team skills (or tactics) develop hand-in-hand. The unique style and flair of each player should be encouraged so as to produce an exciting, appropriately versatile and winning netball team.

Chapter 4

Progressing skills into tactics

Irene Beagles

Irene Beagles *runs her own health and fitness centre. She is an Advanced Coach and life member of Essex Metropolitan County Netball Association. She was England Coach from 1980 to 1983. She has extensive coaching experience from working in the UK and abroad.*

THE NATURE OF TACTICS

A team that understands the principles of the game being played and the strategy of the coach, and which is aware of the tactics of that game, can perform efficiently, confident of success. The importance of team effort and performance is highlighted by B.J. Cratty's statement in *Psychology and Physical Activity* that 'Performance in groups is superior in nearly all cases to performance in isolation. Group members stimulate each other by their very presence and inform each other of the best methods to be utilised. The group holds more past experiences than can be gathered by a single individual working in isolation.' This supports the idea that the whole team as a force against the opposition is more than the sum of the parts – that is, the players.

A feature of good team skill is the application of the correct game plan at the appropriate time within the parameters of the strategy. 'Strategy may be regarded as the management of the tactics and skills of the game' writes Joyce Brown in *Netball the Australian Way*; strategy is long-term planning for perhaps one season, or in preparation for an important competition or championship. For a national team it would certainly represent the planning of the training programme for the World Tournament, but for the netball club or school it may relate to the planning of the programme to improve the position of the club within the league, and the school in relation to the number of matches that should be won in any one year.

Tactics can be defined as the procedure adopted for carrying out a given policy, and in team games may be described as special plans of either attack or defence for a particular match. Tactical plans involve more than one member of a team and are the natural progression from the clever use of individual skill. Good teamwork and correct planning of training programmes should reflect on the netball court when players show capability and confidence, the ability to govern the pace of the play and to make use of advantageous situations, demonstrating flair and skill.

It seems evident that the coaching of tactics should reflect a close relationship between coach and player, and that together they should analyse the information to produce the suitable plans. In team games there is often so much information available to the player that the coach must try to direct or guide the attention of the player to the truly important points in order to make the whole process of decision-making easier. The criterion in the mind of the coach has to be that ultimately the player shall be able to take in the relevant information, process it and make the correct response on her own, and that the role of the coach is one of directing the player to solve the problem.

In any specific game plan which is known and understood by the team, each player undergoes a decision-making process which relates to the ball, the other team players, the space, the conditions and the opposition. The coach, on observing a break-down in the plan, may have to direct the players towards a greater understanding of that process so that an awareness of all that constitutes individual successful performance within the game plan is nurtured and finally achieved. The decision-making process is shown in diagram form in very simple terms in Figure 75.

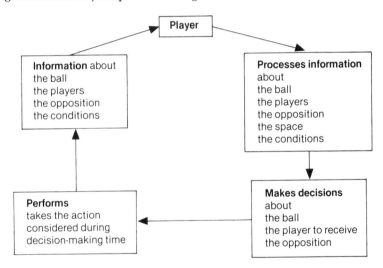

Fig. 75 The decision-making process

As the player becomes more skilful the decision-making process becomes speedier and the performance of the tactic or game plan is enhanced. While Figure 75 shows the factors relating to the process, it may be necessary to define even further the type of information being processed by the player, and Figure 76 shows more precisely what the individual player within the game plan asks herself so that the tactic is performed successfully. The diagram uses only one example of the player who is waiting to play her part in the skilful performance of passing the ball within an attacking game plan, and it should be noted that different situations will demand different questions, but it highlights the coaching point that the process should be 'think-act'.

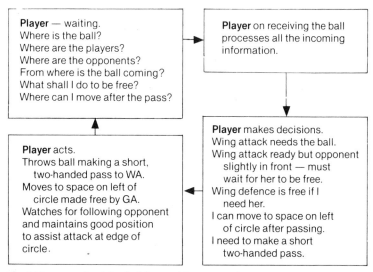

Player — waiting.
Where is the ball?
Where are the players?
Where are the opponents?
From where is the ball coming?
What shall I do to be free?
Where can I move after the pass?

Player on receiving the ball processes all the incoming information.

Player makes decisions.
Wing attack needs the ball.
Wing attack ready but opponent slightly in front — must wait for her to be free.
Wing defence is free if I need her.
I can move to space on left of circle after passing.
I need to make a short two-handed pass.

Player acts.
Throws ball making a short, two-handed pass to WA.
Moves to space on left of circle made free by GA.
Watches for following opponent and maintains good position to assist attack at edge of circle.

Fig. 76 An example of the decision-making process in an attacking move

There is a need here for some explanation as to how tactical plans are arrived at by both the players and the coach. The aim in the long term has to be that in any situation where a problem exists during the netball match, players can solve that problem without direction from the coach. To achieve this aim, the coach has to provide the players with problems of gradually increasing degrees of difficulty, beginning with known and understood situations. For example, in a simple situation in which A is required to pass the ball to B while C defends the pass at the throwing end, as illustrated in the photograph, A may decide to attempt a pass over C, and subsequently may find that C intercepts the pass.

Player A is going to pass to B as C marks the pass

The coach has to ask A all the questions which will enable A to make decisions about the pass to B, thereby solving the problems presented by C. Some of the questions could be

O   where are you holding the ball?
O   where is C?
O   where are her hands – over the ball, around the ball?
O   where is the space around C?
O   is C tall, having a good reach upwards or to the sides?
O   is it possible to make a movement with the ball which will commit C to defend in a particular way, thereby opening up another space through which the ball may pass?

In other words, could player A feint the pass? Horst Wein in *The Science of Hockey* defines the feint or dummy as '. . . a movement designed to mislead the opponent which does not produce the action it suggests. The player for the purpose of concealing his true intentions prepares to perform a certain action, but does not carry it through. Instead he performs a quite different and often quite contradictory one. There are many situations in the course of a game when a feint should be used to gain space or time . . . The dummy therefore, in its most varied forms should be in every player's technical and tactical armoury.' Around any one player there is space through which the ball can be passed. It is impossible for the defending player to cover all those areas at once, but it is increasingly difficult against the player who has developed a repertoire of feints.

The coach can now encourage A to use the space around C to advantage, and perhaps direct her towards recognising the weakness that the tall C may have against the low ball. A simple practice could be set up promoting the use of the 'feint' pass followed by a conditioned game in which maintaining possession of the ball is all important. An example of such a practice is shown in Chapter 3.

As the coach watches the groups of players, she should be assessing the success achieved by each individual.

Since good games skill requires that players can relate to each other efficiently when faced with game problems, they should be coached towards an awareness of how to react to each other having had practice in facing similar recurring game circumstances. Certain players can be grouped together because of the common function they perform during the game. For example Wing Attack, Goal Attack and Goal Shooter are very much involved together in the process of scoring a goal. Sometimes players have specific areas of space to cover, and because of this common theme have to communicate closely in order to perform efficiently. When Goal Keeper is drawn away from the goal-post she should feel confident that the Goal Defence will be aware of the attacking pass to the goal. Similarly, the Goal Shooter who moves away from the goal circle works with the Goal Attack and the coach towards an understanding that, when she moves away, the Goal Attack moves towards the post.

Netball at its best is a fast-moving and dynamic game which causes constant changes in the circumstances of match play, and the problems presented to the players may be many and varied. Some problems may arise frequently while others may happen only once or twice in a game. The coach cannot provide training for all game incidents, but she can provide principles of play which can be used to determine the best possible response. It is the responsibility of the coach to provide these principles along with training in realistic game situations in which the players may practise them. The principles of the game of netball which guide the players can be divided into

O   attacking principles and
O   defending principles

and they are based on the awareness of space, time and action. The ability of any one player to participate in a tactic or game plan is heavily influenced by her knowledge of the techniques involved in the skills to be performed. Without efficient performance of the skills of the game of netball it is almost impossible to realise any tactical move (see Chapter 3). The higher the level of skill, the better the chance of successful tactical play.

Communication between players is an essential feature of tactical plans and can be obtained in a number of ways. In the early stages of developing a tactic, it may be necessary to use a verbal signal to provide the information for the players to decide where, when and how to move. As players become more confident in their understanding of the tactic, information can be provided by a visual signal, or better still by body attitude. While communication is of primary importance, there are a number of factors which remain constant throughout the game of netball.

The *attacking principles* are

O   *possession*, since possession of the ball is of paramount importance in the scoring of a goal
O   *passing*, since the ball can be moved only by a system of passes
O   *availability*, since possession can be safeguarded only when players are available to receive the ball
O   *positioning*, since players must be positioned on the court to allow the ball to be moved
O   *timing*, since the players have to move at the appropriate time to receive the ball
O   *space*, since the ball and the players must have space in which to move

The *defending principles* are

O   *interception*, since repossession of the ball is essential
O   *marking*, since opposing players should not be free to attack
O   *space limitation*, since the opposing players must have difficulty in finding space through which the ball may be passed
O   *goal protection*, since the scoring of a goal by the opposing team must be prevented

While all the points mentioned are important, the two fundamental principles of the game of netball are *possession* and *repossession*.

ATTACKING PRINCIPLES

Use of space

The attacking principles of the game of netball can be maintained only when the players know and understand the role of each playing position, and this in turn needs to be associated with an awareness of court linkage. It is impossible to discuss how the ball can be moved from one player to another in any attacking plan without relating the discussion to the space available to each of the players participating in the plan. The use of the particular player in the attacking plan is appropriate because that player is responsible for the area of space being used. As the ball is passed from the back line through the defending third, then through the centre third and finally into the goal circle, each member of the attacking team will use a particular area of space on the court in which to receive the attacking pass. It should not be necessary to use each player more than once if all team members understand the particular area of space for which they are responsible (see Figure 77).

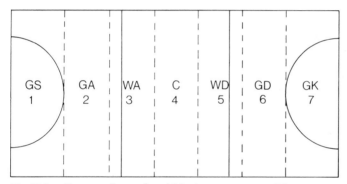

Fig. 77 Specific areas of space for which players are responsible

Initial team spacing is therefore achieved by acknowledging the area of space on court for which each team player is responsible. However, during a game of netball a player may find that she is forced to receive the ball in an area of space for which she is not specifically responsible; for example, if Wing Defence is forced to receive the back-line pass from the Goal Keeper in the band of space for which Goal Defence would normally be responsible. Goal Defence should then be aware, or be directed to be aware, that she should receive the ball in the band of space normally covered by Wing Defence. Goal Defence and Wing Defence have worked a simple interchange with one another. If this court linkage is truly understood by both the coach and the players, much can be done by way of tactical use of the court space with very little planning and few complications. For example, a decision to take a side-line throw-in should relate not so much to who may take it, but to the band of space in which the throw-in is to take place. Figures 78 and 79 illustrate two examples, and show that the use of any player for a side-line throw-in may

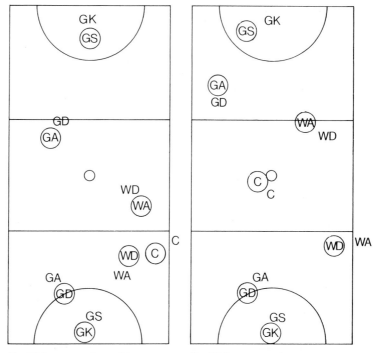

Fig. 78 A congested attacking
space

Fig. 79 Space control

bring about congestion of the attacking space, while the use of the player who is responsible for the specific band of space in which the side-line throw-in is to take place

○   allows the attacking space to be maintained
○   prevents congestion of the attacking space
○   presents to all players an already known attacking move, since it is consistent with the move from the back-line throw-in, and perhaps even in some cases the centre-pass attacking move

There are also very good reasons why the 'free pass' should be played in a similar way, since allowing a player to come forward from her own band of space into one for which she is not responsible could cause a number of opposing players to fill the space in which the player taking the free pass wishes to attack.

It should be noted here that, in spite of the players understanding the use of the court space for which they are responsible, at some stage they need to be introduced to the idea of 'backing up' the player who has just received the ball. A coach who is tactically aware would not encourage her players to pass the ball and run to the space where the ball has been passed, for she would know that, for the ball to be moved in an attacking fashion, space must be created. However, she would encourage her players to pass the ball and then move to either side of the pass they have made, repositioning in an area of the court which would allow the use of a parallel pass, should one be necessary. When the attack breaks down, it may be necessary for the ball to be passed back into an area of space in which 'backing up' players are ready and alert for any eventuality. Most attacking players, having played their part in the attacking move, can retire to their own band of court space, but always with an acute awareness of the positions of the opposing players.

The awareness of the space within the netball court and of how to maintain that space in attack, and of how to close down the space when defending, is possibly the most important feature of tactical team play. It is possible to make some almost clear-cut statements about most of the 'dead-ball' situations which occur in the game; but, since so many situations which occur in the game of netball are never exactly the same, it would be dangerous to imply that such statements should be rules on which to formulate sound tactical plans. However, the information given in Figure 80 on pages 86 and 87 is an attempt to summarise the responsibility of each player within her particular band of space, while at the same time allowing for some degree of interchange when tactically appropriate.

Continuing the previous points made explaining some basic ideas about the use of space associated with court linkage, it is possible to make further suggestions which can assist the coach and players in their appreciation of how space can be maintained and even created. It is difficult to move the ball successfully and safely in space which is congested. For example, defences attempt to confine shooters in one area of the goal circle, making interception possible and giving the shooters problems of 'contact'. Under such conditions it is relatively easy for attacking players attempting the feed pass to make errors of judgement, and in general both the Wing Attack and the Centre dislike the added pressure of the confined space around the shooters. From ideas such as these one can deduce that *crowded space spells danger* for the attacking team.

Assuming that congested space influences the ease of movement by the attacking players, the converse situation – of passing the ball to the player who is alone in space that it unmarked – allows a number of options to the thrower and the receiver. Both players understand that the pass can be taken to the right or the left, that the receiver can run freely to receive the ball, and that the pass should be successful. Thus it can follow that *the lone player in space has the most options.*

The player in space with only one opponent may have to apply her own skill to be free from the defending opponent, but she can still make decisions relatively easily, since the defending player cannot cover all the space around the attacking player simultaneously. The attacking player may be in a position in space early enough to take the initiative, marking the defending player away from the space in which she intends to receive the pass. For example, a Wing Attack may mark the Wing Defence towards the side-line and away from the area of space towards the goal circle.

The shooter who is well positioned in the goal circle, ready to move to

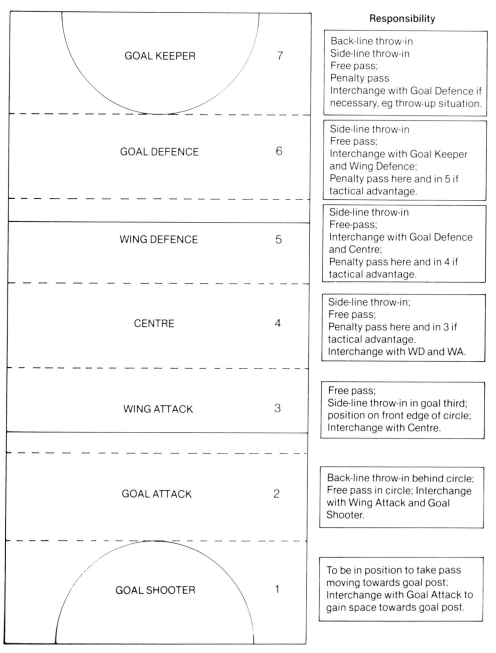

Responsibility

GOAL KEEPER	7	Back-line throw-in Side-line throw-in Free pass; Penalty pass Interchange with Goal Defence if necessary, eg throw-up situation.
GOAL DEFENCE	6	Side-line throw-in Free pass; Interchange with Goal Keeper and Wing Defence; Penalty pass here and in 5 if tactical advantage.
WING DEFENCE	5	Side-line throw-in Free-pass; Interchange with Goal Defence and Centre; Penalty pass here and in 4 if tactical advantage.
CENTRE	4	Side-line throw-in; Free pass; Penalty pass here and in 3 if tactical advantage. Interchange with WD and WA.
WING ATTACK	3	Free pass; Side-line throw-in in goal third; position on front edge of circle; Interchange with Centre.
GOAL ATTACK	2	Back-line throw-in behind circle; Free pass in circle; Interchange with Wing Attack and Goal Shooter.
GOAL SHOOTER	1	To be in position to take pass moving towards goal post; Interchange with Goal Attack to gain space towards goal post.

Fig. 80a This shows the bands of space for which players are responsible and some of the particular responsibilities associated with their roles in these spaces

Common errors	Resulting in
Taking the side-line throw-in in band 6 beyond the front of the circle. Having made the back-line throw-in, enters the court on the same side.	An unprotected goal area; If possession is lost the Goal Shooter may be entirely free at the goal post. Finding herself on the same side as Goal Defence and not available for the parallel pass when necessary.
Taking the side-line throw-in too far into the attacking half of the court. Taking the free pass too far into the attacking half of the court.	Congestion of the attacking space. Failure to be marking opponent should interception by the opposing team take place. Congestion and diminishing space for the attack.
Taking the side-line throw-in in the attacking half of the court. Poor positioning.	Overcrowding of the goal third. Being forced to take a pass which crosses the front of the circle making an interception possible.
Taking the free pass or side-line throw-in in the goal third.	Congestion of the space and forcing the Goal Attack into the goal circle too early.
Using the front corners of the court too often. Not relating to the position of the Centre on the goal circle edge. Not achieving the pass at the centre front circle edge.	Inability to assist in the attack when needed. Overcrowding the same space making passing difficult. A lack of a clear view of the whole circle.
Entering the goal circle too early. Not interchanging with Goal Shooter.	The feed to the circle being more difficult. Loss of the one-on-one situation in the goal circle. Both shooters being on the edge of the goal circle.
Positioning in the space immediately at the goal post. Positioning too near the back line.	Being forced to move away from the goal post to receive the ball. Making the feed ball very difficult.

Fig. 80b The common errors relating to space awareness made by players, and the ensuing results

take the pass towards the goal-post and having only one defending opponent, presents an easier target for the attacking player who is attempting the feed pass into the goal circle. As soon as both Goal Attack and Goal Shooter are in the goal circle with both opposing defences, there is an immediate reduction of the space available to the shooters and for the ball to be passed through by Wing Attack or Centre. If Goal Defence and Goal Keeper drop back to defend the space around Goal Shooter, the Goal Attack becomes the 'long player in space' allowing the use of the 'wall pass' with either Wing Attack or Centre. Occasionally a skilful player may make a successful pass into the goal circle from the centre third of the court, but usually the success of that pass is due to the player's own appreciation of the open space available to the receiver. It is therefore reasonable to say that the skilful player in space with only one opponent should successfully receive the attacking pass.

Frequently a number of players are drawn to the same area of space, making movement and passing difficult, but as one space is congested other areas become free. It is into that free area of space that the ball should then be passed. For example, when Goal Shooter is drawn to the edge of the goal circle and Goal Attack is forced to enter the circle close to Goal Shooter, Wing Attack and Centre have great difficulty in passing the ball to the shooters. It may then be sensible for either Centre or Wing Attack to move speedily to the opposite side of the goal circle to receive a pass away from the crowded space. The Goal Shooter may then be able to turn to receive the pass moving to the goal post. Figure 81 shows an example of this situation and what might happen when the ball is passed into the free space.

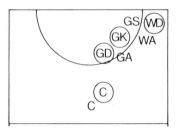 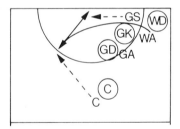

Fig. 81 Showing G S and G A confined on the edge of the circle and the subsequent use of the free space by C to achieve a safe pass to the G S

Figure 82 outlines some of the basic facts relating to the use of space when attacking, and attempts to pinpoint the importance of understanding the tactical use of space. The main headings relate to the key factors governing the use of the attacking space. The subsidiary points relate to the reasons for that statement and cover supporting information for attacking players.

Further examples of space awareness in the goal circle are shown in Figures 83, 84 and 85, which illustrate some instances of where Goal Shooter may move to create space when both Goal Keeper and Goal Defence are

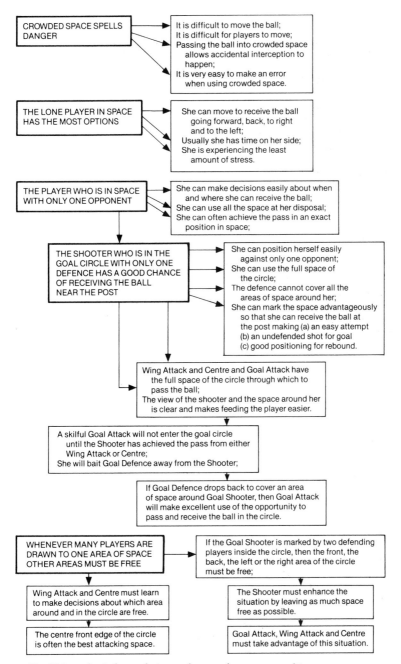

Fig. 82 Some basic facts relating to the use of space — attacking

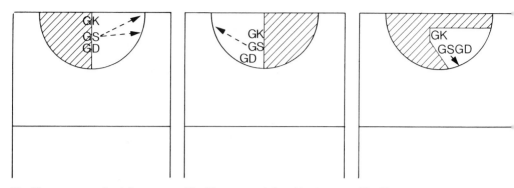

Fig. 83 GS moves to the right of the circle; GA enters the left side of the circle

Fig. 84 GS moves left and back to allow GA to use the right side and the front of the circle

Fig. 85 GS moves right and forward, allowing GA to enter left and deep into the back of the circle

marking her. It should be noted that it is the responsibility of the Goal Shooter to try to clear the space towards the goal-post so that all attacking players are aware of the free space in the goal circle. Furthermore, since the defences are not permitted by the rules to enclose the Goal Shooter so that contact is inevitable, there should always be some freedom for the Goal Shooter to reposition herself.

There are a number of ways in which the Goal Shooter and Goal Attack may combine to outwit tactically the opposing defences, and it seems appropriate to explore some of these methods here.

ATTACKING FOR SHOOTERS

When playing against 'man-to-man' defence

The position of GS in relation to the GK, but more importantly to the goal-post, is decided by the team plan, which is governed by the basic principle of maintaining possession. If the shooter attempts a shot for goal from the edge of the circle, there is obviously more room for error than when taking a close shot. Therefore, it can safely be assumed that both the coach and the shooter should be working towards possession of the ball being taken within 0.9m (3ft) of the goal-post, so that an undefended shot for goal may be taken and almost certainly a goal be scored. Thus the starting position for GS in the goal circle should be away from the post, approximately 2m (6½ft) from the front edge of the circle. The GS should be coached to 'take the initiative' away from the defending GK; all too often the GS thinks of her situation in terms of having to lose the GK before she can receive the ball. Such an attitude is too negative, since the attacking team has possession of the ball, and it is the defending team that has to 'repossess' it. The GS can protect the space to the post by (a) marking the GK away from the post, (b) taking advantage of any outward movement (that is, towards the edge of the circle) by GK, or (c) taking advantage of any positional error by GK; e.g., GK standing squarely behind the GS at all times, or too squarely in front.

The ability of the GS to relate to GA in terms of the space to the post is most important, since the constant interchange of these two players makes defending difficult for the opposing GK and GD. In simple terms it means that, on any occasion that GS is forced to move to the edge of the circle to take possession of the ball, the GA should be aware of her opportunity to run to the post to receive the ball. Simple practices can be used to achieve this, in which the GS within the circle is fed the ball going to the edge, and then immediately passes to the GA who sprints to the post. It should be rehearsed from as many different attitudes as possible around the circle edge and even from the back line. Shooters should be encouraged to make decisions as to which way would be most efficient to turn on receiving the ball in order to safeguard the pass to the incoming attacking player. Variety in the types of pass – e.g., underarm, bounce – should be encouraged, along with differences in the pace of the pass. Accuracy is, of course, of paramount importance.

Individual use of the wall pass or 'in and out' using WA and C should be constantly practised so that, whenever a shooter is double-marked by GK and GD, the GA can gain space towards the post.

Rotation

If WA is required to take a side-line throw-in in the goal third opposite the circle it is possible for the two shooters to set up so that a pass close to the post can finally be achieved (see Figure 86). The WA can pass to the GS, who moves to the edge of the circle. The GS immediately looks for the pass to the GA, who moves towards the post. Even if that pass is not possible, the WA can pass to C, who then looks for the player who is moving towards, not away from, the goal post. The direction of the rotation is governed by the position of GS in relation to GK, since GS cannot push through her opposing GK.

In the situation shown in Figure 87, as the umpire calls 'play' the GS moves towards the post, and it may be possible for WA to make one pass to the post. Alternatively, a pass from WA to C, who delivers a quick underarm pass to the GS, is a possibility.

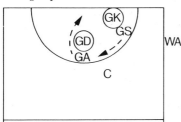

Fig. 86 A side-line throw-in to GS who passes to GA moving to the goal post

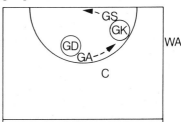

Fig. 87 Rotation towards the goal post

Remember

○   rotation depends on keeping the circular movement going on towards the post
○   rotation works only if both GS and GA are aware of each other and the opposing defence players
○   rotation cannot be set up if both the shooters stay near the goal-post
○   rotation requires communication; that is, GS must call the direction in which both players should move
○   if conditions suddenly change – e.g., the two defences fall back to mark the shooter at the post – the free shooter must use all her knowledge to play the ball with her WA and/or C to break the defence

Screening

If the GS is so positioned in the circle betwen GD and GK that she cannot receive a pass, the GA can run straight at the GD, but then continue her run around the front edge of the circle. One shooter then becomes free as the two defences reposition to cover (see Figure 88).

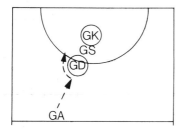

Fig. 88

If GD moves, the front of GS becomes free, and she can move towards the post. If GD stays and GK attempts to pick up GA, then GS becomes free, going towards the post. In both cases the GS acts as a screen to allow the GA to move to the goal-post.

The 'zone' defence in the circle usually represents a loose double-mark by GK and GD on GS and can be difficult to attack. However, it is a good plan to encourage GA to run straight at the centre of the two defences and then to circle the two players to gain the space at the post. The GD may then expect a pass to GA and will often move towards GK, releasing space for GA to move round to the post. Either way, the defence splits allowing one shooter to be free (see Figure 89).

Fig. 89 GA attacks the 'loose double' on GS

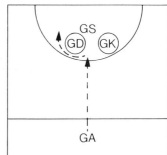

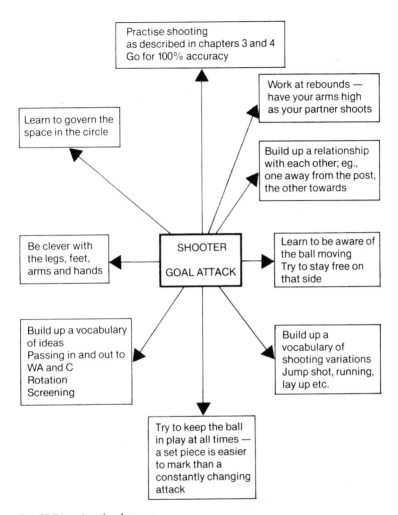

Fig. 90 Directives for shooters

Figure 90 shows the platform of personal skill awareness appropriate to shooters who take part in sound game plans. There is little doubt that without this awareness even the best tactics played in both the centre third and the goal third may break down, causing stress and frustration to the rest of the team. Netball is unique in that it is one of the few games in which only two of the team players are allowed to attempt a shot for goal. It is therefore of paramount importance that these two players shoot accurately and practise frequently all those personal skills which encourage the continued hard work of the rest of the team.

CENTRE PASS

The game of netball is started by a centre pass, and it is at this stage that some reference can be made to set plans or centre-pass tactics, which can guarantee the safe movement of the ball to the goal circle. The choice of which tactical plan to use may be decided by a number of factors which may include

○   the size and height of the team and of the opposition
○   the space available to the attacking players
○   the skill and tactical awareness of the opposition

The tactics which can be applied against an inexperienced team can bring about almost certain success, but the use of tactics is far more pertinent to the game in which the opposition is experienced and skilful. Before the centre-pass plan can be attempted, the team players involved need to be aware of the individual features of their own performance which influence the plan. It is essential that both Wing Attack and Goal Attack come to the centre-third line so that the defending opponents are committed to come forward as well. The attacking Wing Defence and Goal Defence should be ready to take the centre pass should unforeseen circumstances arise which render both the forward players unavailable. All players should be aware of the important role they may have to play to safeguard the attacking space in which the centre pass and subsequent passes to the goal will be made. For example, some opposing Goal Attacks aim to get to the goal-third line as soon as possible after the centre-pass whistle has been blown, to create difficulties for the attacking team, or to mark the forward movement of the attacking Centre. An alert Goal Defence will prevent the continued use of this move by the Goal Attack by marking her closely at the centre pass.

The player who is to receive the centre pass has particular points to remember when going to the line. She needs to be alert with her weight distributed so that she can move at speed suddenly and effectively. She knows that, when she stands at 45° to the line, she can move into the space in which she wishes to receive the ball unmarked. She should know the place where she is intending to receive the ball and, most of all, that she has a vocabulary of methods of getting free so that she can resort to another method should the first plan fail.

Figure 91 shows the Wing Attack ready to take the centre pass and makes reference to some of the points most important to the coach.

The aim of the centre-pass plan is to move the ball from the centre court through the goal third and into the goal circle safely, and to do this it is necessary to understand that it can be safely achieved only when there is no defending opponent between the thrower and the receiver. Furthermore, in any attacking move where three players can move the ball forward with no opposing players between, there is an even greater likelihood of success. To find four attacking players in such a position would suggest that the opposing defences had given up altogether. Seldom is one allowed to set up such a winning triangle of attacking players, particularly at the centre-pass situation, but the coach and the players should be aiming to achieve just that

The player should be alert

Her eyes should be on the ball

She should be standing at 45° to the line

Her weight should be over the leg nearest to her opponent

She should know a number of methods of getting free from her opponent

She should feel ready to move at speed

She should be aware of the space into which she will move to receive the ball

She should be aware of the position of her opponent

She should be aware of the position of the Goal Attack

Fig. 91 Demonstrating centre pass awareness

every time they take possession of the ball. An example of a winning centre-pass triangle is illustrated in Figure 92, which shows clearly the path through which the ball can be moved safely.

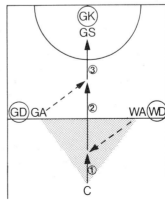

Fig. 92 An unmarked centre pass to shot for goal

However, once the opposing Centre stands in the space in front of the attacking Centre, then the attacking triangle has to be set up somewhat differently; nevertheless, it is still a fact that possession of the ball can be safeguarded only when no defending player is allowed between the thrower and the receiver. Figure 93 shows the safest centre pass using Wing Attack, who passes to Goal Attack who passes to Goal Shooter. The attacking triangle is set up by these three players as they work systematically to take possession of the ball in front of their opposing defending players.

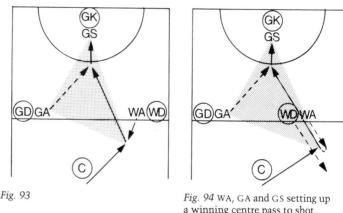

Fig. 93

Fig. 94 WA, GA and GS setting up a winning centre pass to shot for goal

Few opposing defences will allow the Wing Attack and Goal Attack to gain the space they want at the line prior to the centre pass. The Wing Attack usually finds herself on the outside of the Wing Defence and sometimes being forced towards the side line. A skilful Wing Attack will try to capitalise on whatever situation arises, but always with an acute awareness of the need for space. So it is that the next centre pass can be planned using the Wing Attack, who moves onto the ball towards the side-line but who turns in towards Goal Attack after having received the ball. Figure 94 shows once again that a triangle of attacking players has been set up by Wing Attack, Goal Attack and Goal Shooter. The opposing Wing Defence will usually attempt an interception of the pass, and by so doing will clear the space through which the ball can be passed to Goal Attack. Frequently the Wing Attack will find herself marked by both the Wing Defence and the opposing Centre. Knowing that she must safeguard the attacking space, the Wing Attack will encourage the opposing players to move to mark her towards the side-line, thereby clearing the space through the centre of the goal third. Figure 95a shows this game plan and also the attacking triangle set up by Centre, Goal Attack and Goal Shooter.

Therefore, on any occasion when three attacking players are so positioned that the safe passage of the ball is guaranteed, particularly towards the goal, then an attacking triangle has been set up. The more often a team can set up this situation, the greater are the chances of success in moving the

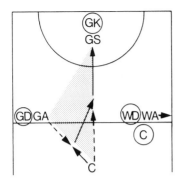

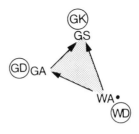

Fig. 95b The attacking triangle set up by WA, GA and GS

Fig. 95a C, GA and GS setting up an attack to goal

ball forward safely. Clearly there are other advantages, since once the triangle is set up it usually allows for an alternative pass to be made. For example, in Figure 95b it is possible for the ball to be passed safely to either Goal Attack or Goal Shooter; Wing Attack may make that decision according to her recognition of the strengths of the opposing players.

It is obvious also that, as soon as one defending player enters the triangle, interception of the pass becomes a possibility. Furthermore, when two defending players are present in the triangle, it is essential to set up a new attacking triangle in a different space. Figure 95c shows the three stages of change involving the attacking move in which interference by the opposing players causes re-establishment of the attacking triangle.

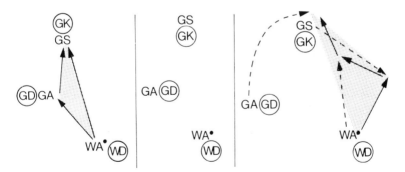

Fig. 95c The re-establishment of the attacking triangle

Figures 96 to 105 describe a number of attacking centre passes which progress to the shot for goal. Coaching points relevant to the plans are listed together with simple practices for receiving the initial pass. A repositioning diagram has been shown in each case to assist both the coach and the player to use the appropriate free space through which to go to the edge of the goal circle.

It can be noted that the final Figures, 104 and 105, show what is the most difficult 'centre pass to shot for goal' sequence, because of the possible interference by the opposing Wing Defence and Goal Defence. However, there are a number of basic tactical principles that apply here; one of the most important might be that, when both the opposing Goal Defence and Wing Defence position themselves between the Wing Attack and the next receiver – in this case the Goal Attack – then it is time for the Goal Shooter to leave the goal circle, thereby coming through the defence to take a pass and allowing Goal Attack to run for the goal circle to attempt a shot.

Some examples of the 'centre pass to shot for goal'

Example 1

Players involved: Wing Attack, Goal Attack, Goal Shooter.

Description of move: Wing Attack and Goal Attack take up a position on court as shown in Figure 96 inside both the defending players. Centre passes

Fig. 96 Movement of players and the repositioning of these players

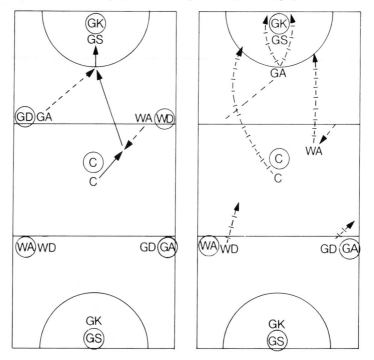

the ball to Wing Attack, who moves in towards the centre of the court. Wing Attack passes to Goal Attack, who times her move to take possession of the ball on the edge of the goal circle. Goal Attack passes to Goal Shooter, who aims to receive the ball moving towards the goal-post.

Repositioning: Centre moves through the space made free by Goal Attack. Wing Attack goes straight to the edge of the goal circle.

Coaching points: Both Wing Attack and Goal Attack should set up a position on the line that suggests either may be taking the centre pass, so that both Wing Defence and Goal Defence are committed to go to the goal-third line to defend. Wing Attack should stand at 45° to the line so that she can sprint unmarked towards the centre of the court.

Wing Attack and Goal Attack should aim to gain as much space as possible, forcing the Wing Defence and the Goal Defence near to the sidelines of the court.

The attacking Wing Defence and Goal Defence should mark the opposing Wing Attack and Goal Attack so that there is no interference by them in the attacking move. The space for the attacking move must be maintained.

Practice: A sets up in a position on the line selected according to all the coaching points set out above. C marks as efficiently as possible. On a signal from B, A sprints to take the pass from B. A may well find that, when the 45° position is efficiently applied, it may not be necessary for her to use speed in going out for the centre pass, and that she may be able to vary her pace considerably.

The coach should encourage A and B to discuss any problems they may find, and to seek solutions for them – reorganising the practice as needed (Figure 97).

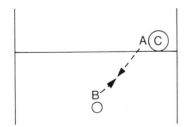

Fig. 97 Centre pass practice

Example 2

Players involved: Wing Attack, Goal Attack, Goal Shooter.

Description of move: Wing Attack and Goal Attack take up a position on the goal-third line as shown in the diagram, Wing Attack being on the outside of the opposing Wing Defence, and Goal Attack being on the inside of the opposing Goal Defence. Centre passes the ball to Wing Attack, who moves out and away from her opponent towards the side-line, taking possession of the ball at a right-angle. Wing Attack passes to Goal Attack, who takes possession approximately at the edge of the goal circle. Goal Attack passes to Goal Shooter, who aims to receive the ball moving towards the goal-post (see Figure 98).

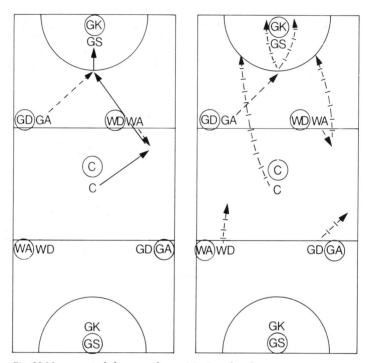

Fig. 98 Movement of players and repositioning after the pass

Repositioning: Centre moves through the space made free by Goal Attack. Wing Attack moves straight to the circle edge.

Coaching points: Both Wing Attack and Goal Attack should set up a position on the goal-third line that suggests that either player may take the centre pass, so that both defending players are committed to the line as well.

Wing Attack should position herself at 45° to the line, as described before.

Wing Attack should aim to gain as much space as possible towards the side-line.

Wing Attack should sprint out from the line, well away from her opponent, to receive the pass at a right-angle to the path of the ball.

Wing Attack should know the area in which she intends to receive the pass.

The attacking Wing Defence and Goal Defence should mark the opposing Wing Attack and Goal Attack away from the centre third, so that any interference by them in the attacking move is prevented.

Wing Attack should attempt to receive the ball landing on her left foot so that she can turn in towards the Goal Attack early.

Practice: A sets up on the line in accordance with all the relevant coaching points stated above. C marks as efficiently as possible. A decides with B the point in the space where the pass should be received. On a signal from B, A sprints to take the pass. D notes the place where the ball was actually received. A and B correct the practice and make the progression to using the fourth player as shown in Figure 99.

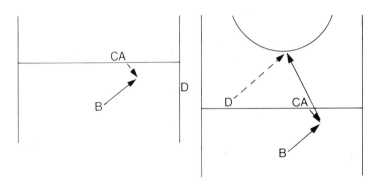

Fig. 99 A simple practice for the centre-pass to WA, with further progression

Example 3

Players involved: Wing Attack, Goal Shooter, Goal Attack.

Description of move: Wing Attack is positioned near the side-lines, having the two opposing defenders on the inside attacking space. Centre passes the ball to Wing Attack, who takes the pass running straight out from the goal-third line. Wing Attack passes to Goal Shooter, who leaves the goal circle, moving left. Goal Shooter passes to Goal Attack, who has sprinted to receive the ball close to the goal-post (Figure 100, page 102).

Repositioning: Wing Attack moves straight to the edge of the goal circle. Centre moves through the space made free by Goal Attack. Goal Shooter uses the space behind the back-line to gain a position at the post.

Coaching points: Both Wing Attack and Goal Attack should take up a position on the goal-third line ready to take a centre pass. Goal Shooter should be alert and aware of the wide position of Wing Attack.

As soon as Wing Attack has moved to receive the centre pass, Goal

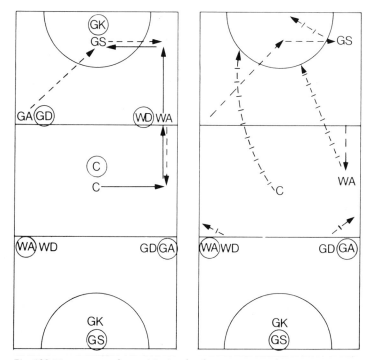

Fig. 100 Movement and repositioning for the centre-pass plan WA, GS, GA

Attack should slip behind the opposing Goal Defence to protect her own route to the goal circle.

Goal Shooter should aim to receive the ball towards her left so that she can either turn in the air or pivot round to face the goal circle as easily as possible.

Wing Attack should use a strong shoulder pass to Goal Shooter (Figure 101).

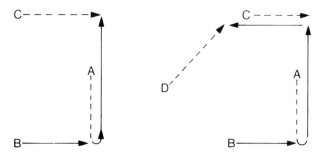

Fig. 101 Centre-pass practice for WA, GS, GA, and progression

Practice: A sprints to receive the pass from B, aiming to turn before landing. A makes a strong shoulder pass to C, who has timed her run to receive the pass at a right-angle to the flight of the ball.

The players progress to the introduction of the fourth player, D, who sprints to receive a pass from C.

Many coaching problems may now evolve; e.g., which is the best way for A *and* for D to turn to receive the pass?

Defending players can be introduced gradually until the practice becomes almost like the game situation.

Example 4

Players involved: Goal Attack, Wing Attack, Goal Shooter.

Description of move: Wing Attack is efficiently marked by Wing Defence and Centre, so that she cannot receive the centre pass safely. Wing Attack safeguards the centre space by taking the two defending players as wide as possible.

Centre passes to Goal Attack and moves straight through the middle of the goal third to receive the return pass from Goal Attack. Centre then passes to Goal Shooter, who aims to take possession moving towards the goal-post (Figure 102).

Repositioning: Wing Attack moves straight to the goal-circle edge. Goal Attack moves towards the circle using her own side of the court (Figure 102).

Fig. 102 C, GA, GS centre-pass with diagram of repositioning for these players

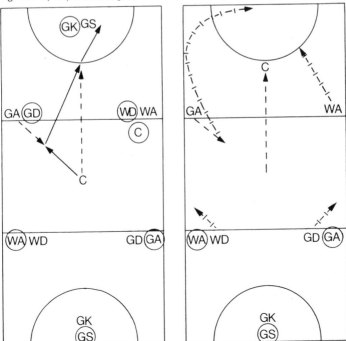

Coaching Points: Wing Attack should try to clear the centre space by moving as wide as possible while still occupying the opposing Centre and Wing Defence.

Centre should be ready to sprint through the middle space to receive the return pass from Goal Attack.

Goal Attack should aim to come out for the centre pass well clear of her opposing Goal Defence.

Goal Attack should look for the opportunity to use a fast return pass to Centre.

Fig. 103 A practice for the first return pass between C and GA

Practice: A sprints to take a pass from B and quickly releases the return pass to B as she moves forward. B bounces the ball to C in a controlled manner (Figure 103).

The practice can be progressed by introducing the defending players and by varying the pass to C.

The aim is to achieve a fast release to B and involves the 'catch-throw' technique.

Example 5

Players involved: Wing Attack, Goal Attack, Goal Shooter.

Description of move: Wing Attack is forced to take up a position towards the side-line outside the Wing Defence.

Centre passes to Wing Attack, who moves towards the side-line. When Wing Attack receives the ball she frequently finds that both Wing Defence and Goal Defence are between her and the attacking Goal Attack, so a pass to the edge of the goal circle could be intercepted. It is possible to solve the problem by encouraging Goal Attack to sprint for the circle edge, but then to make a sudden change of direction, thereby ridding herself of the Wing Defence. The Goal Attack is then able to receive the pass from Wing Attack in a more central position so that she can pass to Goal Shooter, who is in the goal circle (Figure 104).

An alternative plan (see Figure 105) is possible if Wing Attack moves out

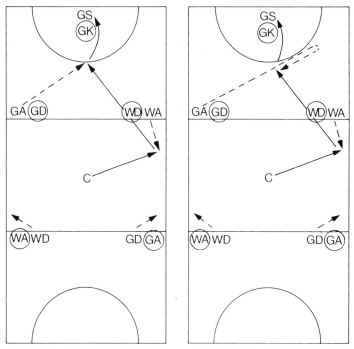

Fig. 104

Fig. 105 (below) The alternative plan in which GA moves round the GD, followed by the repositioning of the players

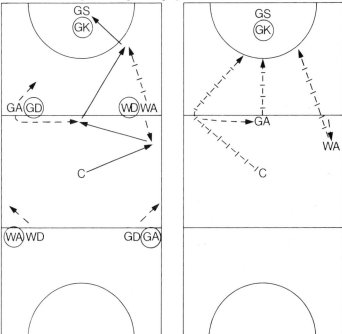

to receive the pass from Centre. Goal Attack moves towards the goal circle, then checks and changes direction coming round the opposing Goal Defence to take possession of the ball in the region of the goal-third line. The Goal Attack then looks for a fast wall pass to Wing Attack, who passes the ball into the goal circle to Goal Shooter.

BACK-LINE THROW-IN

Having achieved the 'centre pass to shot for goal' game plan successfully, the next step has to be the side-line throw-in to shot for goal, followed by the back-line throw-in. The side-line throw-in has been dealt with earlier and should not present any difficulty if both players and coach relate it to court linkage.

While the same may be said of the back-line throw-in, the exact positionings of the players should be related first of all to the awareness of the basic tactical rule that the ball should be moved away from the opponents' attacking goal and towards one's own attacking goal. It may also be noted here that the players need to stand off the space in which they wish to receive the ball, so that they may move onto the ball as it progresses through the court. Figure 106 shows the path of the ball from the back line to the goal-post, and it can be seen both that all seven players have been used in this game plan, and that the ball has not passed in front of the opponents' attacking goal. Figure 107 shows the position in which each player takes possession of the ball and relates closely to the awareness of court linkage.

So that the players shall achieve possession of the ball in the space most advantageous to the attacking move, they need to be aware of where to start. Figure 108 shows both the starting position and the movement of the players in the attacking plan.

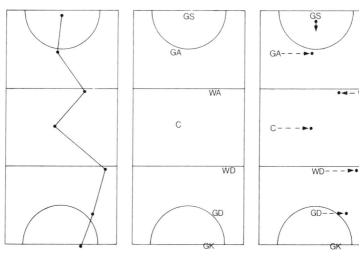

Fig. 106 This shows the path of the ball from the back line

Fig. 107 Showing the position in which the players receive the ball

Fig. 108 Showing the movement of the players

There are many variations to such plans, and it would be impossible to show all of them here. However, the basic principles of court linkage and maintenance of both space and possession of the ball remain constant. As players become more skilful and more confident they may well find that it is possible to pass the ball across the goal circle occasionally, but only when that is the space which is completely free of any opponent, and when it is infinitely safe.

It would be easy here to make no further comment on the back-line throw-in plan, but one of the problems that seems to present itself constantly

Fig. 109 This shows the path taken by each player to reposition herself in an advantageous area of space after she has passed the ball

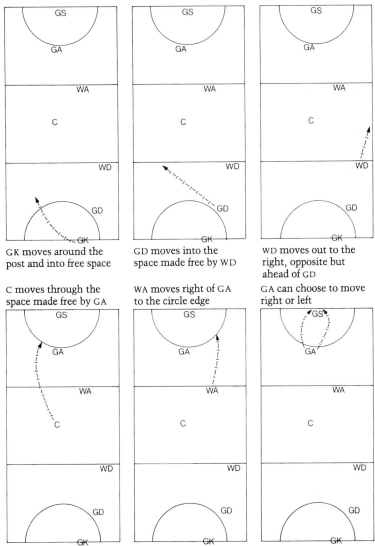

GK moves around the post and into free space

C moves through the space made free by GA

GD moves into the space made free by WD

WA moves right of GA to the circle edge

WD moves out to the right, opposite but ahead of GD

GA can choose to move right or left

is the repositioning of players after they have played their part in the attacking move.

Figure 109 attempts to show where each player may reposition herself in the most advantageous area of space after she has passed the ball. Once again, there is a need for the coach to reinforce the point that a player should not follow the path of her own pass and that what she is really trying to achieve, in repositioning, is a follow-up movement which will make her available for another pass, should it be necessary. Furthermore, in understanding repositioning the player becomes useful without causing any problems for her team-mates.

Figure 110 shows an example of the back-line throw-in when Goal Defence is marked by both Goal Attack and Goal Shooter. In this case, the Wing Defence takes the first pass from Goal Keeper while Goal Defence attempts to move away from that space, clearing a path for Goal Keeper to join in the attacking move. Centre moves to take a pass from Wing Defence while Goal Defence sprints towards the attacking goal-third line to take her first pass. The rest of the attacking move is completed by the Wing Attack, Goal Attack and Goal Shooter with no further interchange. Figure 111 shows the path described by the ball during this attacking move.

Fig. 110 Back line throw-in when GD is marked by GS and GA, showing the movement of the players

Fig. 111 Showing the path of the ball during the attacking move as in *Fig. 110*

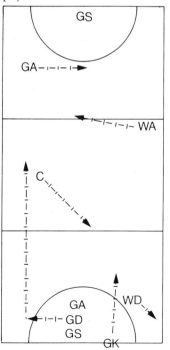

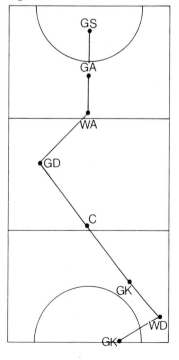

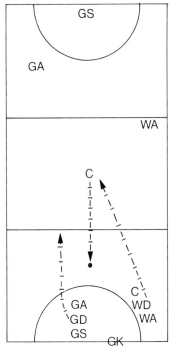

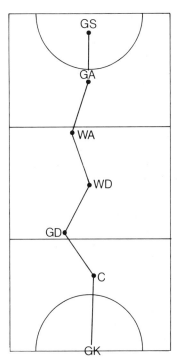

Fig. 112 Showing the movement of players

Fig. 113 Showing the path of the ball

There are occasions when both Goal Defence and Wing Defence are each marked by two opposing players, making the back-line throw-in more difficult. However, it is possible to move the ball safely if space is maintained and sufficient thought is given to the movement of the players. Figures 112 and 113 show that it is possible for Centre to take the first pass from Goal Keeper while Goal Defence and Wing Defence move away from the centre area of the defending third, clearing the path for the pass.

This is not a plan for beginning netball players, since it requires a good understanding of interchange and use of court space. Furthermore, the ball will be passed through the opponents' attacking goal circle, and it has already been stated that the basic plan of moving the ball away from the opponents' attacking goal area should be encouraged.

TACTICAL DEFENDING

'In defence . . . here we are involved in restricting space through which and into which attacking players can move with safety. The defence attempts to restrict the gaps through which passes can be made,' wrote Alan Wade in *The F.A. Guide to Training and Coaching.*

The basic skill of marking the player has been defined in earlier chapters, along with the further stages of marking the pass and lastly the space through which either the ball or the player may pass. The application of those skills, along with the control of the overall space, is what governs the composition of tactical plans for defence.

First of all it is necessary to understand some basic facts which relate to efficient defending. Since opening up space is so important in successful attacking, the converse – that is, the 'closing down' or filling of space – is of immense importance in defence. This suggests that, although a player may have marked her opponent efficiently enough to prevent her from receiving a pass, there is more that she can do to assist in defence. The Wing Attack and Goal Attack who realise that they can fill the space on their opponents' goal-third line, with the possibility of gaining an interception as well, are showing a good level of tactical awareness.

A coach has to make decisions about the method of defence she should use; that is, either man-to-man, zone or space defence or a careful combination of both. As the match progresses, she may decide to make slight changes, which could include spending two defending players on one attacking player who has shown a high level of success consistently throughout the game. Whatever she decides or whatever she has practised with the players, she will attempt to create in her players an ability to assess their opponents' weaknesses, and to make a concentrated effort to capitalise on them. She will encourage her players to apply the type of marking which disrupts the flow of the attack, and stress that such situations as a set piece (for example, a sideline throw-in) are easier to defend than an uninterrupted, well timed attacking move. Just as a coach will encourge her attacking players to keep the ball in play when on the attack, so too will she encourage the players when on the defensive to put the ball out of play.

She will urge her players to confine the attack in limited space as often as possible, and will set up practice situations to use such skills as reverse pivot, in which the Goal Defence controls the movement of the Goal Attack in her approach to the goal circle. Figure 114 shows the opposing Goal Attack

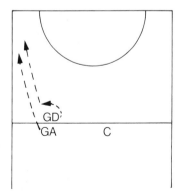

Fig. 114 The use of reverse pivot by GD

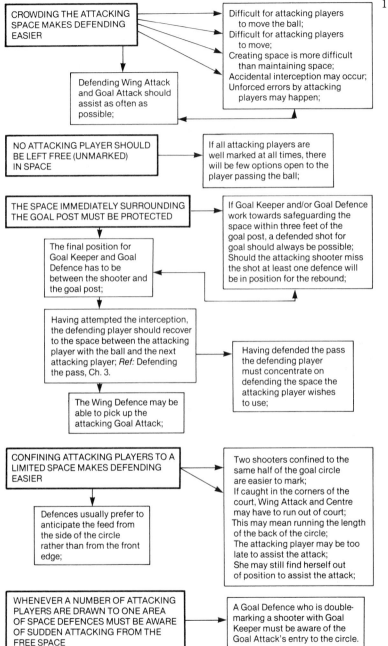

CROWDING THE ATTACKING SPACE MAKES DEFENDING EASIER

Difficult for attacking players to move the ball;
Difficult for attacking players to move;
Creating space is more difficult than maintaining space;
Accidental interception may occur;
Unforced errors by attacking players may happen;

Defending Wing Attack and Goal Attack should assist as often as possible;

NO ATTACKING PLAYER SHOULD BE LEFT FREE (UNMARKED) IN SPACE

If all attacking players are well marked at all times, there will be few options open to the player passing the ball;

THE SPACE IMMEDIATELY SURROUNDING THE GOAL POST MUST BE PROTECTED

If Goal Keeper and/or Goal Defence work towards safeguarding the space within three feet of the goal post, a defended shot for goal should always be possible; Should the attacking shooter miss the shot at least one defence will be in position for the rebound;

The final position for Goal Keeper and Goal Defence has to be between the shooter and the goal post;

Having attempted the interception, the defending player should recover to the space between the attacking player with the ball and the next attacking player; Ref: Defending the pass, Ch. 3.

Having defended the pass the defending player must concentrate on defending the space the attacking player wishes to use;

The Wing Defence may be able to pick up the attacking Goal Attack;

CONFINING ATTACKING PLAYERS TO A LIMITED SPACE MAKES DEFENDING EASIER

Two shooters confined to the same half of the goal circle are easier to mark;
If caught in the corners of the court, Wing Attack and Centre may have to run out of court; This may mean running the length of the back of the circle;
The attacking player may be too late to assist the attack;
She may still find herself out of position to assist the attack;

Defences usually prefer to anticipate the feed from the side of the circle rather than from the front edge;

WHENEVER A NUMBER OF ATTACKING PLAYERS ARE DRAWN TO ONE AREA OF SPACE DEFENCES MUST BE AWARE OF SUDDEN ATTACKING FROM THE FREE SPACE

A Goal Defence who is double-marking a shooter with Goal Keeper must be aware of the Goal Attack's entry to the circle.

Fig. 115 Some basic facts relating to the use of space — defending

moving towards the goal circle. Goal Defence is marking the space through which the Goal Attack wishes to move. As soon as the attacking player is level and about to pass Goal Defence, it is necessary for the defending player to reverse pivot – in this case on her right foot – to force the Goal Attack to move out and away from the goal circle. The reverse pivot allows the Goal Defence to be facing the on-coming attacking pass when it is made and thus there may arise an opportunity for interception. Whatever the coach and the players decide is the tactical game plan, it is obvious that repossession of the ball is the objective.

The main headings in Figure 115 pinpoint some of the more important facts which relate to the application of good man-to-man defence. The subsidiary information attempts to explain briefly why these points are so important. The Figure is intended as a guide to coaches, and may help in building up a gradual awareness of sound defence in the players. Parts of the Figure could be used to draw up a chart for display for school players.

Zone defence

While man-to-man defence can be very effective, it is necessary to have other tactical plans of defence available when competing against very skilful players who make few errors. The use of *zone defence* may be applicable here, and it may well represent the sudden tactical change which causes the opponents to reassess and alter their pattern of attack.

The aim of zoning is to defend an area of space, closing down those areas of space through which the ball may pass and thereby making an interception of the ball possible. It can be successfully employed against a team which shows a lack of variety in attacking game plans and where its efficient use of the skills of the game is suspect. Zoning seems to cause confusion among attacking players because there seems to be so little space in which to move the ball, but there are a number of reasons why it is not as efficient as the man-to-man system of defence.

Zoning in the defending third is most common, and is set up by placing the Goal Keeper, Goal Defence, Wing Defence and Centre in the defending third. Goal Keeper and Goal Defence cover the area close to the goal-post, while Wing Defence and Centre are positioned on the edge of the goal circle, ready to move to close the gaps in the space through which the ball could pass (see Figure 116).

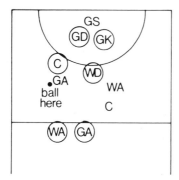

Fig. 116 Zone defence in the opposing goal third

'The basic philosophy of Zone Defence is that every player is responsible for a designated defensive floor area, primarily determined by the position of the ball,' wrote Bob Cousy and Frank Power in *Basketball Concepts and Techniques*. It is vitally important that the players involved in the zone understand that concentration on the ball is the key to success. Players in the zone must ignore the attackers and at no time be tempted to break the formation and leave a gap through which the ball could be passed successfully. As the ball is moved by the attackers, so too the zone moves to cover the passage of the ball. Where there is a high level of communication between the members of the zone there is usually a high degree of success, for the Goal Keeper and Goal Defence who are positioned within the circle can see the danger areas more readily. The timing of the defending-third zone is important, for if it is set up too early it gives the attacking team a very easy time through the mid-court space. As a guide to timing, the zone should be set up as the ball is moved into the defending third.

A variation of this particular zone-defence plan is sometimes used. As the ball is brought into the defending third by the attacking team, the Goal Keeper and Goal Defence cover the space in the goal circle while either Centre or Wing Defence cover the crown of the goal circle, according to the position of the ball. For example, if Wing Attack takes possession of the ball, then Centre moves to cover the space at the crown of the circle while Wing Defence covers the pass to be attempted by Wing Attack. If Goal Attack is given the ball, then Centre moves towards her to cover the pass while Wing Defence moves to cover the space on the crown of the circle (see Figure 117). It should be noted that Centre and Wing Defence do not overlap each other but work to cover the space, each one understanding the floor area they should cover in relation to the position of the ball (see Figure 118).

Fig. 117 Zone defence: in this case using C on the crown of the circle and WD covering the pass

Fig. 118 Repositioning of C and WD as the ball is moved from one side of the court to the other

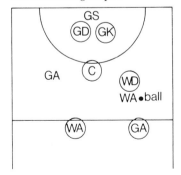 

There are various patterns of zone defence and it is possible to set up a zone in the centre third, but it requires considerable coordination of the defending players and constant concentration and discipline. It is usually set

up by using Goal Attack, Centre and Wing Defence as a wall across the centre of the middle third. It is timed to come into action as soon as the opposing team have gained possession in their defending third. Once again, the aim is to close down the mid-court space to both the attacking players and the movement of the ball, aiming for interceptions to be made. Goal Defence, Wing Attack and Goal Shooter assist by preventing the free movement of other attacking players into the zoned area (see Figure 119).

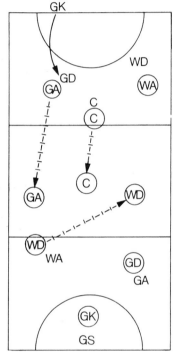

Fig. 119 A mid-court zone defence

This is an exciting game plan since it sets up a barrier of players across the court, but it relies heavily on the players' ability to intercept the ball and is therefore vulnerable if there is any lack of concentration by the defending players. It can also be broken by constant attacking at the sides and by encouraging the attacking players to keep possession, almost baiting the zone players and then suddenly breaking through. The clever attacking Goal Shooter who may be very mobile can also upset the plan, for she may well leave the goal circle to receive a pass in space which has been sent over the zone from the centre third. The Goal Attack may then find that she has a free run to the goal circle.

It is of course also possible for the attacking team to send players on a dummy run so that the defence believes that the ball will be passed into that space. The defence may then react to the dummy, so that space for the pass is created.

To summarise:

O   zone defence is effective only when all players defend the space; players should learn to concentrate on watching the ball, not the attacking players

O   players should understand the importance of closing down the space through which the ball may be passed and how this can be achieved

O   players should understand how the space is covered and that they should not overlap each other

O   players should appreciate the importance of maintaining the zone formation and not be tempted to react carelessly

In netball it is not possible to use all seven players in the team to set up a zone in any one third of the court, since there are space limitations on the players. It should therefore be noted that to attempt to cover the width and the depth of the court simultaneously is almost impossible. It is probably better to select either width or depth; further work on this has been done by Sally Dewhurst-Hands in *Netball – A Tactical Approach*.

Defending tactics at the centre-pass situation

There are other defending tactics apart from man-to-man and zone defence which can assist the defending team in their aim to repossess the ball. At the centre pass, the attacking Goal Attack and Wing Attack will usually try to achieve an inside position on the third line. Most skilful defending players will pre-empt this by marking the two attacking players before they can take up a position on the line. However, if the Goal Attack and Wing Attack win the position on the line it is possible for the defending centre to drop back towards the third line to cover the pass to either attacker (see Figure 120).

Fig. 120 C defending on the third line

Fig. 121 C and WD marking WA

There are times when the Wing Attack is consistently successful in achieving the centre pass even when she is forced to receive the ball moving out towards the side-line of the court. It may be useful on this occasion to spend another player – i.e., the defending Centre – on marking the front of the Wing Attack so that she is unable to achieve the centre pass safely. It may also prove to be a tactical advantage to force the Goal Attack into the centre third to take the pass, for this allows more time for the Goal Defence to cover the space through which the Goal Attack wishes to approach the goal circle (see Figure 121).

To assist the successful application of the tactics, it is necessary for the defending Goal Attack and Wing Attack to mark their opponents at the centre pass, so that the alternative pass to either of these two players is not available to the attacking Centre.

Defending the side-line throw-in

Assuming that all defending players are aware of the importance of marking their opponents, it is possible to use some variations which may produce either interceptions or errors on the part of the attacking team. Figure 122 illustrates 'overloading'. The defending Goal Attack and Wing Attack have moved into the space near the goal-third line and towards the throw-in. The defending Centre has taken up a position in front of the attacking Centre to mark the pass. All other defending players have set up in front of their attacking opponents and are aware of the opportunities to intercept any forward pass from the attacking Centre. In this situation the only safe passes are to Wing Defence or Goal Defence, and these cannot be achieved easily in the attacking space.

When a team has assessed the performance of the opponents, it may be thought necessary to limit the skill of the attacking team by double-marking the most skilful players, particularly when they are positioned in advantageous attacking spaces. Figure 123 shows the defending Wing Defence and

Fig. 122 Showing 'overload'

Fig. 123 Double marking of two attacking players

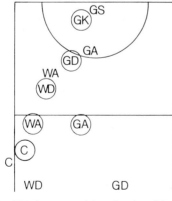
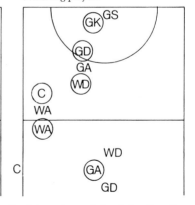

Goal Defence marking the attacking Goal Attack, and the defending Centre and Wing Attack marking the attacking Wing Attack. The defending Goal Attack is attempting to cover a pass to either Wing Defence or Goal Defence. In this tactical plan it can be seen that the attacking Centre will have some difficulty in achieving a forward pass.

Conclusions on defence

During a netball match players will make decisions with the coach about when to use particular defending tactics, and it is obvious that the wide vocabulary of tactical plans allows a team to switch from one plan to another, forcing constant readjustment on the part of the attacking team.

Finally, it can be seen that tactical defence is impossible in a team in which the players are not building up the constant application of those skills which allow the tactical plan to be successful. Figure 124 attempts to set out some of the basic points which both Goal Defence and Goal Keeper should remember throughout the netball match.

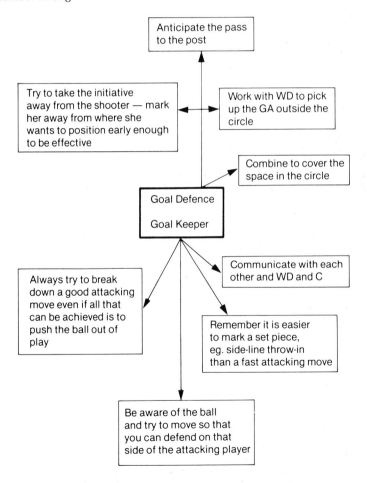

Fig. 124 Basic points to be noted for efficient tactical defence

Chapter 5

The role of the coach

Sylvia Eastley

Sylvia Eastley *is probably best known for her years as Editor of the*
A E N A Netball *magazine, an ex-international umpire and past Chairman
of the* A E N A *Umpiring Sub-committee. She is an Advanced Coach,
having coached the Bedfordshire Senior County Squad for eight years.
She is a member of the National Executive Committee and East Region
Council.*

It would be impossible to discuss either the functions or the duties of a
coach under one heading, since there are numerous facets of her role.

The purpose of this chapter is to identify the areas which a coach will
need to consider if she is to perform her role effectively. I have assumed that
the coach has sufficient technical knowledge to meet the requirements of the
group she is to coach.

Personal qualities

Coaching is a personalised way of imparting knowledge. No two coaches
are alike – the style which suits one may be totally unsuitable for another –
indicating that the coach should develop a style which is natural to her. But
there appear to be certain traits about the successful coach which are
desirable, regardless of the style employed, such as understanding (of
players), enthusiasm, self-discipline, determination, ability to motivate,
tolerance and a sense of humour.

Responsibilities towards her players

The main responsibility of the coach is to develop the maximum
potential and ability within each player, and the ways in which she can
facilitate this are numerous.

Teacher

The presentation of material should be clear, simple and concise. Lack of
improvement can often be blamed on the number of complex instructions
issued at one time. A coach is responsible for educating her players and she
should encourage them to play with understanding, not being afraid to ask
questions whenever necessary. The coach will need also to be responsible for
training the captain in her duties (see Chapter 13).

There may also be instances when a coach is required to work with an assistant, possibly one who is to be her ultimate replacement. Much thought will need to be given to helping her to develop not only her skills but also her coaching style and her role within the squad.

Leader

As leader of her group, the coach will be responsible for discipline both on and off the court. Her own standards of discipline should be rigidly adhered to, and the same should be demanded from her players.

Counsellor

This is a most important duty of a coach, especially when dealing with young players. She should always be prepared to lend an ear to a problem, although care must be taken not to be seen as favouring a chosen few. She should learn when to be sympathetic, when to be brisk, and when not to listen at all.

Organiser

Coaching requires an orderly and methodical approach at all times, whether it is in the administration or in the practical elements of the game. With regard to the actual training session, it is only the foolish coach who will attempt it with no preparation (see below).

Trainer

Any form of strenuous activity requires the body to be adequately prepared, and netball, with its explosive bursts of speed, high leaps and twists and turns in the air, is no exception.

The type of fitness training will depend on the expected level of competition. The coach should be inventive with the fitness programme so that it is enjoyed rather than tolerated (see Chapter 7).

Exemplar

The personal standards of dress, behaviour and attitude of the coach go a long way towards determining those of her players, and play an important part in team morale. The coach should be aware of the image she presents.

Adjudicator

This is possibly the most difficult duty for a coach to perform since it clashes with certain of the other duties. She will be required to evaluate and select on the basis of that evaluation, and the job must be tackled with objectivity and integrity.

Administrator

If a coach is expected to keep records of attendance, dispersal of kit, analysis of performance records, payment of cash and so on, she should be aware that this is time-consuming, and allocate time either before or after the actual training session.

Pre-organisation of a training session

As stated earlier, the coach is expected to be thorough in her approach to organisation – otherwise, the pitfalls are numerous.

Facilities

The first consideration has to be whether the session is to take place indoors or outside. If outdoors, the coach should make sure that the players are dressed suitably for the prevailing weather conditions.

Where indoor facilities are small, perhaps the first part of the session, to take in fitness training and skills practices, could be spent inside, using a full-size outdoor court for the game situation.

Equipment

Netballs should be pumped up before the session commences – ideally there should be one ball per player, but one between three ought to be the absolute minimum. Other equipment includes: bibs/bands, skittles, circuit equipment, and audiovisual aids.

If court areas need marking out for a specific practice, this should be done before the training session and not taken out of training time.

Outline of session

If every second of practice time is to be used to effect, a plan for the session is required. The less experienced coach will need to note the practices she intends to use, as well as the timing of each part of the session. However, it is not always possible to stick to time factors, since the rate of progress of the players should be the criterion which determines when the coach moves on to the next part of the practice.

Techniques of coaching

The basic techniques of coaching do not vary a great deal from sport to sport, and certain guidelines have evolved which allow both coach and player to receive maximum benefits from the session. Slow progress can often be a result of poor technique on the part of the coach, not because her material is at fault but because the players have not understood what is being asked of them.

Positioning of the coach

The position of the coach in relation to the group is important. Valuable time and energy can be wasted if the coach stands in the middle of the group, so that the players behind cannot hear or see her.

The position of the sun in relation to the group is another factor which is often forgotten. The sun should be in the eyes of the coach and not those of the players, or all the hard work of the demonstration will be wasted.

The acoustics of some sports halls are poor. Keeping the players in a compact group around the coach when talking can diminish the echo effect.

Demonstrations

Demonstrations should be kept as clear and simple as possible, although there are many different types, each with different advantages and requiring different approaches.

O   If performed by the coach, the demonstration can be executed in a slow, exaggerated fashion. It is sometimes helpful after the initial demonstration to select a player to allow the skill to be displayed at normal speed.

O   If a player is selected to demonstrate, the coach will need to give verbal guidance to the viewers to direct their attention to particular aspects of the demonstration.

O   In certain situations, usually when the movements are particularly difficult, the coach may need to demonstrate a point by mechanically guiding the limbs of the player through the movements.

O   When setting up a group practice it can be more easily and quickly understood if a 'guinea pig' group is used to show how the practice is to work.

O   A tactical situation can be explained more easily by a demonstration. The route the ball will take should be shown, as well as the starting points and the follow-up positions of the players.

Verbal instructions

Verbal instructions should be concise and clear and given in a method-ical, not haphazard, fashion.

The voice should be expressive and vital, since the easiest way of 'switching off' players is to talk in a continuous flat, monotonous tone. The coach must ensure that the players are familiar with her terminology – 'third stage marking' may mean something to the coach but be meaningless to the players.

Refinement of a skill

The technique of skill teaching can vary. The more rigid approach, where the coaching points are given accompanied by a demonstration, leading immediately into small-group work, can be effective, especially when dealing with experienced players, capable of assimilating verbal information easily.

However, the less experienced player, not used to translating words into action, could find a more flexible approach more beneficial. Using this technique, players are given the minimum of verbal instruction, allowing them to be active immediately, performing the skill in a rough fashion. Once they have become familiar with the skill, the practice is stopped and a few coaching points are given so that the rough form may be improved upon, and the skill become more effective. Finally the key coaching points are given and the skill is then performed in its refined form, ultimately moving through the normal developmental practices.

Group membership

When considering the membership of her groups, the coach will need to take into account not only the skill level of her players but psychological factors, too (see Chapter 8).

Some coaches feel that players with similar abilities should be grouped together, while others feel equally strongly that players of mixed ability should form the basis for group structure. There are no hard and fast rules on the matter, as there are advantages and disadvantages in both methods.

Placement of groups

An orderly and methodical approach to group organisation can make life easier for the coach as well as for the players. Rather than allowing the groups to set themselves up in a scattered fashion, it is sometimes useful to use the divisions of the court or any lines that are marked out. By having the practices working in the same direction, it can be much easier to observe progress throughout the groups – and it is frequently safer (see Figure 125).

Coaching the groups

The coach should visit each group in turn, helping individuals when required, and giving feedback to all players at some point. There is a danger of neglecting those players who are coping adequately.

If a particular fault is common to all groups, the practice should be stopped and the coaching points reiterated before proceeding. A watchful eye should be kept on the timing of the practice and progression made as soon as the skill is mastered. Practices which are allowed to continue long after the skill is perfected can quickly become boring, causing quality of performance to drop.

Coaching in the game situation

For the new coach, this is possibly the most difficult part of coaching. Everything in the game is happening at speed and the mind can easily go blank, making it impossible to utter a word.

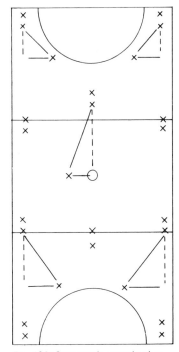

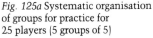

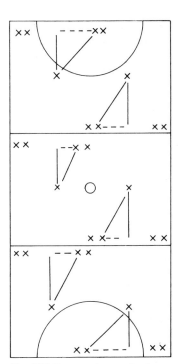

Fig. 125a Systematic organisation
of groups for practice for
25 players (5 groups of 5)

Fig. 125b Systematic organisation
of groups for practice for
30 players (6 groups of 5)

The secret is total involvement and perhaps, initially, to make comments on what she sees rather than to attempt to coach. There may be a need simply to practise voice projection and display self-confidence.

Once the hurdle has been crossed, this is the area where the coach can be relaxed and uninhibited, with the players responding to her advice and instructions and even to the inflection of her voice. A middle line should be adopted where the coach is neither barraging the players with constant chatter nor expecting them to react to thought-transference.

Coaching in the game becomes erratic and frustrating if the specific coaching point is left until the skill has actually broken down. The coach should attempt to foresee the problem before it occurs and 'talk' the player through it. For example, when coaching the skill of balance and control on landing, the coach should give the key coaching points as the player is about to take off for the ball, rather than when she has landed.

Encouragement and praise should be given readily, although blanket praise, regardless of whether it is deserved or not, soon becomes meaningless to the players.

When a skill or tactic breaks down, the coach should not be hesitant about stopping the game. As with praise, coaching too becomes meaningless if faults are not corrected or brought to the player's notice.

Enthusiasm, drive and involvement are important features of coaching in the game if the coach is to motivate her players.

The conditioned game

A conditioned game is a game which the coach controls by instigating her own rules to allow maximum opportunity for a skill or a tactic to be performed.

Having coached a skill, a normal game often provides too few ideal opportunities for the coach to see if the coaching has been assimilated and is being put to good use.

The conditioning could be achieved by removing aspects of the game which interfere with the execution of the skill. For example, assuming that the skill of throwing has been coached, its execution would be made easier by removing any defending of the thrower. A further example might be the case of the throw-up skill. Instead of waiting for a simultaneous offence to happen, a throw-up could be taken each time the ball went out of court, or perhaps instead of a centre pass.

Another form of conditioning is to give a free pass to the opposition each time the skill breaks down.

The coach can devise many ways of conditioning the game to suit her requirements, but she must always ensure that the players understand the condition of the particular game.

Coaching in the match game

Coaching in the match game varies considerably from coaching in the practice game. The rules of netball do not allow coaching from the side-lines. Advice and constructive criticism have to be left until the intervals of the match, when comments must be clear and concise, as time is short. Some coaches find it helpful to keep a notebook to hand and jot down the points which they will need to clarify during the interval.

Conclusion

After reading this chapter, one thing should be clear: there is more to coaching than simply standing on a side-line, shouting at players. One has to work at becoming a good coach. It does not just happen.

Chapter 6
Planning a coaching programme
Phyl Edwards

Phyl Edwards, M.A., is a sport consultant with an interest in applying information technology and management theory to sport. She represented England in the 1967 Netball World Tournament. She was also Assistant England Netball Coach from 1976 to 1977, is a squash panel tutor and coach and a senior athletics coach. Her coaching experience is extensive both in the UK and abroad. She is the author of several publications relating to such diverse areas as sports science, centres of excellence, and squash.

Whether a coach is preparing for a new coaching post, a new season, or even the World Tournament, the activities which she will undertake are very similar. In doing so the coach is acting in the role of a manager, and as such is responsible not only for ensuring that her team are mentally and physically prepared for the level of competition in which they are to participate, but also for the total efficient running of her team. As a manager, therefore, she is responsible for *strategic planning*, a continuous process which is illustrated in Figure 126 below.

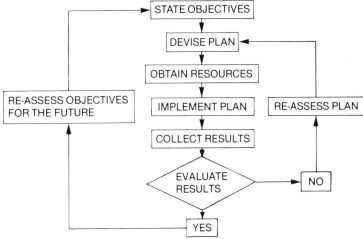

Fig. 126

Objectives

The statement of objectives is absolutely essential before developing a coaching programme. Unless a coach knows exactly what she wants to achieve, she is in danger of dissipating her own and her team's energies to no very clear end.

Objectives are highly specific statements about what is to be achieved. They must have a timescale, and there should be an indication of what they are going to cost in terms of resources – financial, temporal and physical.

A coach may start the season with several objectives which she might put in a rank order. For example:

1   to improve the overall fitness of her team by 25% by the first week in October
2   to cut down on the tactical and skill errors of her team by a measurable amount (for example, 10%) by Christmas
3   to improve or maintain her team's league position by the end of the season
4   to win her league's end-of-season tournament on a specific date

The above are clearly stated, measurable objectives, and have specific timetables for achievement. However, whether or not they are realistic will depend on such factors as

O   the innate ability of the players in the team
O   the motivation of players and coach
O   the resources available in terms of money, facilities and time

It is essential that the coach assesses realistically all the variables which are likely to influence the achievement of her objectives before finalising her goals.

To achieve objectives, a plan of action must be formulated. Plans can cover any time period: they may be for a season or for a specific event, the main differences being in the amount of detail and complexity included – i.e., the long-term plan will be expressed in more general terms than those for a specific event.

DEVISING A PLAN (1):
PLANNING FOR A SEASON

Unless starting completely from scratch, the coach would be well advised to establish at the end of the previous season a list of those players who are intending to attend trials for the following season. During the off season she should try to ensure that any new players moving into the area are aware of the existence of her club. This could be achieved by sending letters to all the local schools' PE departments, advertising in the local press, and placing notices in sport and recreation centres.

Obtain resources

Logistics

Before the season starts, the coach should check thoroughly that all logistical problems are anticipated, even if not actually solved. They may include:

O booking facilities for practices and matches
O checking *all* equipment, and repairing or replacing as necessary
O liaising with committee members with regard to any administrative matters which might influence her role; for example, trials notifications or the amount of money available to pay for such things as hire of courts

Insurance

This may involve advising players with regard to the advantages of personal accident or private medical insurance. In the event of injury players so covered will have access to, for example, physiotherapy treatment much quicker than through the normal NHS channels. However, it must not be forgotten that referral by a GP is normally obligatory.

Further to this, the coach should check on public liability insurance, especially with regard to the use of hired courts. The terms of the Health and Safety at Work Act should also be considered when working in school/college gyms and local authority centres. While litigation is not yet the norm in the UK, coaches are reminded of recent claims made in the High Court against coaches of gymnastics and trampolining.

Finally, it is also advisable to investigate the possible adverse effect car-sharing might have on a driver's insurance policy. Where 'petrol money' is accepted, it may be that a claim following an accident could be prejudiced by the car having, in legal terms, been 'hired out'.

Implementing the plan

The coach's plan for the season could be represented in overall terms as in the table below.

Table 1: *The seasonal plan*

Training period	Time spent on physical fitness %	Time spent on technical training %
Transitional	75	25
Early season	60	40
Mid-season	35	65
High season	25	75

The level and intensity of work will be dependent upon whether the coach is a teacher dealing with school teams, a club coach, or the county or national coach. However, while the total content itself will be different, the ratios will remain the same.

Transition period

This involves the general physical preparation of the players, with the emphasis being put on fitness. During this time the training load is increased as the players' fitness increases.

Example:

Match play: no competitive netball

Physical preparation	55% of each session
Technical preparation	25% of each session
Tactical preparation	20% of each session

Mid-season

This stage has the players involved in a great deal of competitive play and, hence, they should be fit enough to sustain their skills. Therefore the emphasis swings from fitness training to training in the skills and tactics of the game.

Example:

Match play: competitive matches

Physical preparation	25% of each session
Technical preparation	45% of each session
Tactical preparation	30% of each session

High season

The full competition programme is reaching a climax. League positions are established, tournament matches are being played and end-of-season tournament dates are being prepared for. Now the emphasis is very heavily on the tactics, with the other aspects supporting this work.

Example:

Match play: full competitive matches

Physical preparation	10% of each session
Technical preparation	15% of each session
Tactical preparation	75% of each session

Collection of results and evaluation

At the end of the season the coach should collect together all the results she has achieved throughout the year. These should include not only the results of matches, but also all the many other measurable parts of her work. For example:

○ numbers of players leaving or joining the club throughout the year, with reasons in the case of leavers
○ the incidence of injury to players throughout the year, with when and how the injuries occurred, plus comments on possible reasons (e.g., poor surface, player unfit) as well as the length of time the player was out of the game
○ attendance at practices, with comments on possible reasons for rises and falls in attendance
○ a brief overview of each player's strengths/weaknesses which might act as a guideline for next season's planning

An evaluation of her results provides the feedback by which she judges whether or not she has achieved her stated objectives. Success may mean an increase in the level she wishes to attain in the following year. Failure may mean she must either rethink her objectives, which may have been unrealistically high, or re-think her plan and its implementation. The feedback process is essential and *must* be carried out if team planning is going to be a dynamic process and not just a 'dead end' each year.

DEVISING A PLAN (2):
PLANNING FOR A SPECIFIC EVENT

The preparation of the team for match play is a vital part of a coach's strategy. It does not matter how fit or how skilful the team: if they fail in the competitive situation, all the preparation counts for nothing. Most teams at club and even county level take each match as it comes, with little forethought as to *exactly* what is likely to face them in a given situation. To prepare for competition the planning can be subdivided into three areas of preparation:

○ pre-event
○ in-event
○ post-event

Pre-event preparation

Before sending her team into a competitive situation the coach should attempt to learn as much as possible about their prospective opponents. This should involve such information as:

○ the composition of the opposing team in terms of
  player positions
  player sizes
  handedness
  fitness levels
○ the strength and weakness of the opposition in terms of attack and
  defence tactics
○ such psychological factors as might be applicable; e.g.,
  players who 'crack' under pressure
  players who fight to the end
  players who excel at set pieces; e.g.,
    throw-ups and penalties

The opposition is composed not only of players but of a coach and umpire who should also be taken into account. For example, how authoritarian is the coach? Does she expect her team to stick to her game plan or will she allow them to make their own decisions? How dependent on her are the team – will their performance drop in her absence? By the same token, if it is known that the opposition's umpire will be controlling the game, then a profile of her should be built up by the coach. For example, does she have any idiosyncrasies in her umpiring style which might adversely affect the performance of the coach's team? If the answer to this is 'yes', then the team should be prepared for this in practice and not meet the problem for the first time in the competitive situation.

Pre-event preparation such as this should help to

○ take advantage of the opposition's weaknesses
○ neutralise their strong points
○ compensate for any weaknesses your team might have
○ optimise your team's own strengths

The collection of information with regard to opponents is an accepted fact of life in such sports as soccer, basketball and track and field. As yet, in netball it is an area which has received little attention. Scouting is always considered to occur only in the professional sport, and where it involves much time and travel this is undoubtedly true. Video analysis of the opposition's last league game is not a realistic option for the average netball coach. However, there is nothing to stop her, the umpire and the team building up a dossier on opponents, their grounds and their officials. This may be done in a formal manner by the use of match-analysis sheets (Figure 127), which may be subjected to statistical scrutiny over a period of time. More likely is the use of a series of personal notes which can be kept by individuals and pooled either in written form or by word of mouth.

Part of a coach's remit in pre-match preparation includes training her team in simulated match conditions. As early as possible before a given event, the coach should try to ascertain all the relevant conditions which are likely to affect her team's performance and create conditions in training as similar as possible to those anticipated in the competition.

Quarters	Penalties				Inaccurate passes				Throw-ups ✓ = won x = loss				Foot faults				Dropped passes				Unforced errors			
	1	2	3	4	1	2	3	4	1	2	3	4	1	2	3	4	1	2	3	4	1	2	3	4
GS																								
GA																								
WA																								
C																								
WD																								
GD																								
GK																								
Total:																								
Mean ($\bar{x}$)																								

Fig. 127 Match analysis

Possibly the easiest condition to simulate is the number and length of games to be played in a tournament. She should know if they will have to play successive matches or if they have a rest – and, if so, for how long. As soon as possible she should have assessed who will be the most difficult opposition and where they will come in relation to the total tournament.

A coach should always be helping her team to judge time, a vital aspect of netball, which is a very temporally bound game. Players should be able to judge three seconds, fifteen minutes, ten minutes or whatever timespan is applicable to the competition. For example, it may be vital to 'freeze' the game in the last few minutes before half-time to ensure retaining a centre pass. To do this effectively players *must* be able to judge time. The coach herself must be able to judge time, particularly player-deterioration time: she should be able to judge, particularly in extended tournament conditions, when a player has reached a stage of fatigue which argues against her continuing to participate.

Another aspect of time which is important is the time of day at which players are to be asked to play. Not all players play well, for example, very early in the morning. While the coach cannot readily change the players' biological rhythms, she can at least attempt to prepare their system for the shock by holding practices at the time they will have to play.

The climatic and environmental conditions should also be simulated as far as possible. If a team is to compete outside, then part of their training should also be outside. If it is known that they will have to play on a different surface than that to which they are accustomed – for example, some of the synthetic surfaces found in different sport centres – then the coach should attempt to let them have some practice on a similar ground. It must be remembered that the nature of the interface between the shoe and the playing surface will differ according to the materials from which both are constructed. This factor may not only adversely affect the player's skill but also contribute towards the risk of injury.

Finally, the coach should try to simulate in practice the type of opposition tactics her team is likely to encounter. She should develop in her players the skill of 'reading' the game and of making adjustments in their play to cope with different opposition tactics. They should be taught how to deal with various types of zone defence, with very tight man-to-man defence or double-blocks on certain players. Whatever they are likely to encounter in competition should have been practised in training.

In the final run up to the competition the coach should ensure that

○ each individual player is as prepared as she can be – i.e., fit, free from injury and illness, and with her skill at as high a level as possible
○ each player is aware of her tactical role and team responsibility
○ players know all the arrangements for travel, accommodation, site of venue, etc., and that they have a 'phone number to contact in case of emergency
○ the players understand any rules specific to the event in which they are to participate

The coach should ensure that just before the competition her players have 'peaked' in terms of fitness and can be 'tapered off' in final preparation. This will mean that for at least *two* days ahead of an important competition they will do no hard training, nor play any competitive matches. They should come to competition physically fit, mentally relaxed and 'hungry' for competition.

The event

Pre-event tactics

The coach should ensure that all the players arrive at the venue well ahead of the start of the event so that there is time to hold a team meeting before the start of play. This should be short but give the coach an opportunity to state very clearly exactly what she expects from team and individuals and to give them encouragement and, one hopes, confidence.

The team warm-up

Players should start their warm-up at least half an hour before the event. It should include a vigorous physical warm-up, the practice of specific individual and unit skills, and a run-through of set-pieces and tactics. The warm-up should prepare the team physically and mentally for competition. Following this, the coach should allow the team approximately 5 – 7 minutes between the end of the warm-up and the start of the event. More than this and the effects of the warm-up will have begun to wear off; less and the team will be still recovering. Therefore it is critical that the coach gets her timing correct.

In-event tactics

While the coach cannot actively coach her team during play, breaks in play for quarter- and half-time afford an opportunity for her to communicate with the team. At these times she should provide them with feedback concerning performance, instructions with regard to tactics (i.e., whether to continue with the set plan or adjust the prepared tactics) and finally encouragement. How the coach does this will depend on such factors as the relationship she has with her team, and whether they are winning or losing, playing well or badly. The coach should be prepared to make justifiable criticisms, but should temper these according to the situation. However it is done, feedback must be obtained and used as a measure of whether or not the coach has achieved her objectives.

Post-event tactics

Analysis and evaluation

Without feedback, learning and hence improvement will not take place. Whatever the coach does with her team should be analysed and the results of this analysis compared with what she had intended to achieve. 'Feedback loops' should exist throughout the system. Certain forms of feedback are intrinsic to the activity – e.g., a goal is scored or not scored. However, this feedback is made more meaningful when it is augmented by information from the coach, who tells the player *why* she was successful or not. In certain situations the coach can give feedback immediately; for example, during a training session. At other times the feedback must be delayed and given by the coach at half- or quarter-time, or at the end of the match. Whenever or however it is done, *feedback must be provided.*

In a match, where activity is happening very quickly and where more than one player is involved, analysis is very difficult. Also it must be remembered that in these situations a degree of subjectivity occurs; that is, it becomes a matter of personal opinion. The coach should always try to make her analysis as objective as possible, concentrating on activities such as goals attempted and gained, number of penalties given away, and number of foot faults committed. These are relatively simple analyses to make, and can be facilitated by keeping match-analysis sheets. These sheets may be completed by players 'on the bench', although in this case 'operator error' is likely to occur. Obviously one of the best methods of analysis is through the use of a video film of match play or individual skills. This method can provide both immediate feedback, *via* the 'instant replay' and a final analysis made by watching the match at some time after the event.

However it is done, feedback *must* be obtained and used as a measure of whether or not the coach has achieved her objectives. If the coach trains herself to keep records of *relevant* facts, she will find it an invaluable help in her on-going preparation and planning, as well as in terms of future developments.

PLANNING A COACHING SESSION

Planning should precede any organised sport activity and, therefore, no matter how often the coach works with her team each individual session should be carefully planned. Remember: *winning is the science of being totally prepared* and this preparedness applies to training as much as to competition.

The venue

Unless the club has a regular booking for the venue and is, therefore, given precedence over other users, the coach would be well advised to confirm that the facility is actually available at the times which she has planned. Further to this, she should know that the facility which is at her disposal is suited to the activity she wishes to undertake. For example, if she intends to test the team's endurance fitness by using the Harvard Step Test she must ensure that sufficient benches or chairs of a suitable height are available.

The equipment

All the equipment the coach intends to use should be in appropriate order, and this fact must be checked before the start of the session. Balls should be inflated before the start of training: this should not be the first job for players on arriving at the court. The bibs or bands should be in the relevant team units, so that players can quickly select the appropriate colour and cut down on loss of playing time. Stopwatches should be fully wound and, as far as the coach can tell, giving an accurate reading. The well organised coach will not only have remembered her whistle but will probably have a spare in case of emergency. Finally, any other equipment which the coach intends to use must be available and checked *before* the players arrive.

Time

The coach should always arrive before the players. This means that she can go through her pretraining check-list before the commencement of the session. Most clubs hire their facilities, and therefore have made a financial commitment in the form of the hiring fee: it seems, therefore, inappropriate that any of the time for which the club has paid should be used for purposes other than the coaching and playing of netball. *Coach/player time is work time*; it is not administration time, nor is it the time for socialising. Both of these activities are necessary and desirable for the efficient operation of a club, but they should be undertaken at a time other than team practice. Therefore, as soon as the players arrive on the court – *work begins.*

Session plan

Each coaching session should have an objective or goal which the coach wishes to achieve during practice time. This means that the coach should have planned before coming to the session exactly what she intends to do to achieve her goal. Having said this, it does not mean that the plan cannot contain a great deal of flexibility; the true art of coaching is knowing the correct thing to do at the correct time, and this may be completely unplanned.

Depending upon the level of competence and experience of the coach, she will draw up a session plan for each practice. The content of the session will depend upon the stage in the season in which it is taking place and, therefore, where she is placing her emphasis; i.e., on fitness, skill or tactics. However, as a general rule the type of plan a coach might adopt for a mid-season session could be as follows:

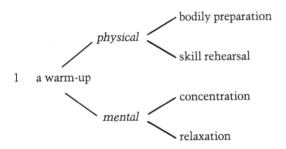

1   a warm-up

2   a game – for observation by the coach and re-familiarisation by the players
3   a technique, skill and tactical coaching period
4   a conditioned game
5   possibly, and where necessary, more work out of the game
6   a further conditioned game
7   a full game

How much detail a coach puts into her plan will depend on various factors:

O   *her level of experience.* The coach who is just starting her career may need to make a very detailed plan for herself to follow during the session. This is useful, but has the inherent risk of her continuing to pursue the plan irrespective of whether it is what the team needs at that moment. The more experienced coach may merely plan the warm-up and then base her coaching on what she observes are the team's immediate needs.

O   *the background to the session.* In this case the coaching session may be a direct follow-up to a specific competitive game. The coach, on the basis of either observation or statistical analysis, might have decided that a certain area of play was failing in competition. In this case she will plan exactly what she has to do to correct the fault and create possible improvements in play.

The plan

The coach has, then, a specific objective which she wishes to achieve in a given session. While the skeleton of her session plan will remain constant, the content will change in line with this objective.

An example of the type of plan which might be appropriate for a club side during the season is exemplified below.

1   Warm-up
(time: approximately 10 minutes)

O   jogging
O   stretching
O   speed work
O   technique and mental preparation

2   A game
(time: approximately 10 minutes)

In the normal adult club situation the coach should use the whole/part/whole method of presentation. By this is meant that

1   The teams play a normal competitive game.
2   The coach observes play and, based on her judgement of the performance,
3   selects the area of maximum weakness and takes that *part* out of the *whole*. Having isolated it, she attempts to correct faults or develop strengths. This may be done by practising techniques, skills, unit skills or set-piece tactics.
4   Following a period of isolated practice the parts are returned once again to the *whole* game.

3   Technique, skill, tactical work
(time: approximately 20 – 30 minutes)

During this period the coach will

1   break down the aspect of play that she is to work on
2   analyse the basic principles
3   provide the players with information regarding how their performance differs from the ideal
4   set corrective practices
5   provide feedback to the players with regard to their performance
6   reinforce correct responses and generally motivate the team to work hard both physically and mentally during what is frequently an arduous and difficult period

4 Conditioned game
(time: approximately 10 minutes)

In this game the coach lays down her 'rules' of play. For example, a team which has been working on ball-handling techniques and skills might have the condition imposed that every pass which in the coach's opinion is either incorrectly executed or an inappropriate selection results in a loss of possession and a free pass to the opposing team.

5 Full game
(time: dependent upon length of session, or the degree of success of the preceding work)

Hopefully, the coach will now be able to coach in the game, stopping only as appropriate to comment, correct or reinforce her coaching points. However, should it be necessary steps 3 and 4 (above) may be repeated. Now is the time when the coach will simulate competition. This may be with respect to the length of the game: for example, where the team is preparing for a tournament which involves many short games, the remainder of the time may be used to play competitive games of the appropriate length with suitable periods of rest between each. Following the end of the game the players should warm-down by jogging gently for approximately five minutes.

6 Discussion

Every session should end with the coach and players getting together to discuss any aspects of relevance. These may relate to the session just completed, the game in general, or any problems encountered by the players either in or out of the game.

This is an important part of the session as it brings the group together as a unit. It allows players to talk and express opinions, and possibly to ask for explanation or clarification of points they may not have understood. It also allows the coach time to give any instructions necessary about training to be done before the next session or details regarding the next fixture. Finally, it may give the coach a further insight into her players' personalities and possibly highlight any individual problems which may be adversely affecting team performance.

CONCLUSION

Planning is essential for success. It is, unfortunately, an area rarely discussed in coach-education programmes; yet without it the coach is in danger of wasting her own and other people's time. Therefore, it is essential that, as well as acquiring a knowledge of the techniques, skills and tactics of the game, the coach should also acquire the skill of planning as an essential part of her education.

Chapter 7

Physiological considerations

Sue Campbell

Sue Campbell, M. ED. *is the Deputy Director of the National Coaching Foundation. She played netball for England at Under-21 and Senior level. She was also a junior international athlete. She is an Advanced Coach and umpire. She has also been Coach to the British Universities Netball Team, as well as Team Manager to the England Women's Basketball Team and to the England Universities Women's Athletics Team. She is a* B A A B *senior coach.*

THE FUNCTIONING BODY

The human body is a complex unit consisting of various systems. As with a car engine, the more regularly it is serviced and tuned the better it will run. It is possible for a car to survive without servicing if all you want it to do is crawl down to the local shops, but if you want it to compete in a rally then you have to tune the engine.

The heart

The heart is the body's engine, and the fitness of the cardiac (heart) muscle may determine the way a player performs. There is no short cut to fitness, but with careful preparation and planning the fitness road can be a straight and relatively pleasant one. The pulse rate (heart beat) is a good indication of fitness and the effects of training. Every player should be taught to take their own pulse rate and use it to measure their individual response to exercise (see photograph).

The heart is influenced by many factors, including posture, exercise, emotion and body temperature. The normal heart rate under resting conditions is about 78 beats per minute for men and 84 beats per minute for women. The heart rate diminishes progressively from birth to adolescence but increases slightly again in old age.

When exercise begins, the heart rate increases. The speed and intensity of this rise will depend on the type of exercise (its intensity and duration), the emotional content of the exercise, the environmental temperature and humidity, and the physical condition of the subject. The rapidity with which the heart rate returns to normal at the cessation of exercise is often used as a test of cardiovascular fitness. In players in good physical condition, recovery occurs more rapidly than in poorly trained players. During exercise the increased oxygen requirement of the contracting muscles is met by an increased flow of blood through the muscles. This is made possible by an increase in the amount of blood pumped by the heart and by circulatory adjustments.

One of the most important factors that limits human physical performance is the ability to increase cardiac output. The heart rate responds to light or moderate exercise-loads with a rapid increase to a plateau. The rate is proportional to the work load and to the oxygen consumption. In very heavy exercise, the rate continues to increase without levelling off, until exhaustion ends the work bout. (See Figure 128.)

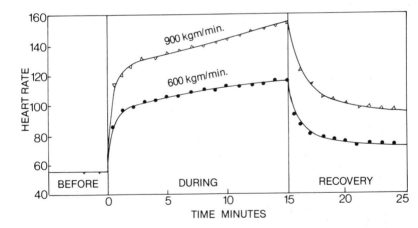

Fig. 128 Changes in heart rate in the same moderately-conditioned person at workloads of 600 and 900 kgm/min

The heart rate responds differently to different types of exercise. In general, dynamic muscular activity brings about a much greater increase in heart rate than static, straining types of exercise. Consequently, when preparing a fitness programme for netball players it is important to include plenty of dynamic activities as these will bring about a more rapid improvement in endurance (stamina) than static work. Athletic training brings about changes in heart rate, stroke volume and other factors, all of which interact to bring about a more effective and efficient adjustment of the player to exercise.

Respiration

Respiration, in the broadest sense of the word, includes all the processes that contribute to the exchange of gases between an organism and the environment. All animal tissues – even at rest – require a continuous supply of oxygen and the continuous removal of carbon dioxide. Exercise increases both of these needs.

The lungs are ventilated at rhythmic intervals to replace the oxygen that has been absorbed into the blood and to remove the carbon dioxide that has been liberated from the blood. The volume of air drawn into the lungs at each inspiration and expelled at each expiration is referred to as the *tidal volume*. During quiet breathing this is about 500ml (about 17½fl oz), but it increases rapidly in exercise.

When an individual begins to exercise, the body metabolism increases and consequently there is a greater need for oxygen. Each 100ml (about 3½fl oz) of arterial blood contains on average about 20ml (about ¾fl oz) of oxygen. The oxygen is carried by the pigment haemoglobin to the working muscle. As an individual begins to work, the muscles involved in the extra exertion demand more fuel. There is an increase in blood flow through the lungs, where the blood is saturated with oxygen and then transmitted to the muscle.

The total respiratory process consists of three component functions: gas exchange in the lungs, gas transport to the tissues by the blood, and gas exchange between the blood and the tissue fluids bathing the cells. Air flow into and out of the lungs depends upon the differences of pressure between the ambient air and the air within the lung.

This pressure gradient is brought about by the muscular activity of the diaphragm and intercostals in normal resting breathing (see Figure 129). The

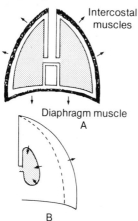

Intercostal muscles

Diaphragm muscle
A

B
Pneumothorax

Fig. 129a Inspiration is brought about by the descent of the diaphragm and the movement of the chest wall upwards and outwards. Expiration is brought about by the elastic recoil of the lungs and the chest wall.

Fig. 129b When air enters the pleural cavity (pneumothorax) the chest wall moves outwards and the lungs collapse inwards.

work of breathing is relatively small at rest. During vigorous exercise, extra oxygen is made available by increasing the rate of breathing.

Exercise metabolism

In the normal resting individual, the supply of oxygen to the tissues is sufficient for its needs. During light exercise, if there is still adequate oxygen, the carbohydrate sources of energy in the muscle are completely oxidised to carbon dioxide and water, thereby producing the energy needed for muscular activity. For a short period of time – often during heavy exercise – muscular activity can also be supplied with energy from anaerobic processes (processes occurring without oxygen).

One of the by-products of anaerobic exercise is lactic acid, which can cause problems when it accumulates in the muscle. When adequate oxygen supplies are available, a complete breakdown of glycogen occurs and there is no accumulation of lactic acid. When exercise creates the need for more oxygen than can be supplied by the cardiorespiratory processes, part of the energy for muscular activity is supplied by the anaerobic mechanism, and lactic acid accumulates as the end product of metabolism. Whenever the supply of oxygen is insufficient to meet demands an individual is said to contract an *oxygen debt.*

In light exercise, where a steady state is achieved, only a small oxygen debt occurs and this is paid off in a few minutes. When an exercise represents a true overload, the duration of the effort is limited by the player's ability to accept an oxygen debt. This oxygen debt is repaid during the recovery period by consumption of more oxygen per minute than would normally be consumed in a resting state. It is interesting for netballers to note that, when equal loads of continuous and intermittent work are compared, much lower oxygen debts seem to result from intermittent work. This knowledge can help the coach to prepare an appropriate training schedule. It is unlikely that players will incur a very high oxygen debt during a netball match due to the intermittent work pattern, but the players must still have good endurance to maintain their level of performance throughout a full game.

It has been suggested that, if physical fitness is defined as the capacity for doing work, the best single measure of this factor is maximal oxygen consumption (the maximum amount of oxygen capable of being transported and utilised by the working muscles). An individual's vital capacity may be measured by well tried and tested techniques. The difficulty in netball is to gather data on the type and intensity of work which players undertake during a match. The apparatus which needs to be fitted to the players can be distracting and cumbersome. Some research has been carried out, but there is still much to be done before training schedules can claim to be based on scientific facts rather than intelligent guesswork.

TRAINING FOR NETBALL

There are many factors to be included when designing a training programme for netball players. Consideration needs to be given to the 's' factors: stamina, strength, suppleness, speed, skill and psychology. Two of these – skill and psychology – are dealt with in other chapters and will here be referred to only briefly, but they are an integral part of a player's preparation.

Strength refers to the capacity of muscles to exert force. In netball, short explosive bursts of power and *speed* are necessary, and consequently increased strength results in improved performance – jumping higher, throwing harder, moving more dynamically.

Stamina, or cardiorespiratory endurance, is essential if players are to sustain intense activity throughout the game. Good endurance is dependent upon efficient respiratory, cardiac and circulatory functions, and it can be improved by regular, vigorous training which causes a noticeable increase in heart rate (approximately double the resting pulse rate – or more).

Suppleness refers to the range of motion of the joints. This is essential if players are to be mobile on court and it might provide a reach advantage over a less flexible opponent. Slow static stretch has been found to improve flexibility and – unlike strength and endurance activities – these exercises are best done slowly, avoiding rapid, bouncing motions.

Physical improvements may be brought about through training. L. Brouha has identified some of these functional improvements as follows:

○ increased muscular strength
○ greater maximal oxygen consumption
○ higher maximum cardiac output – greater volume of blood pumped by the heart and less of an increase in pulse rate and blood pressure during submaximal exercise
○ more economical lung ventilation during exercise and a greater maximum lung ventilation
○ increased capacity to perform more work aerobically, thereby decreasing the tendency to incur an oxygen debt and lactic acid build-up, which causes fatigue
○ quicker recovery in pulse rate and blood pressure after exercise
○ better heat dissipation during exercise

Principles of training

Certain basic principles must be followed if a sensible training schedule is to be devised. The most crucial factor to remember is that adaptation to training is very specific. Consequently, to improve power, a player must do strengthening exercises; to increase stamina, endurance work must be done; and stretching exercises are necessary to extend the range of movement. The training programme has to be comprehensive in content and include activities that place strength, endurance and flexibility stressors on the individual if the player is to achieve her maximum potential.

Overload

If the session is to have the required effect, then the particular activity being performed must exceed either in intensity or duration the demands regularly encountered by the player. Too much overload can cause pain, but if a player is going to improve she must tax her present capacity.

Progression

As a player's capacity for work increases, greater demands must be made if improvement is to continue. Consequently training schedules need to be reviewed frequently and individual targets set according to personal needs.

Regularity

All players should train regularly and those involved at high competitive levels should have a daily work-out. Even when a high level of fitness has been achieved the player cannot afford to stop working. Fitness soon fades! Nevertheless, it is true that maintaining fitness is easier than attaining it in the first place.

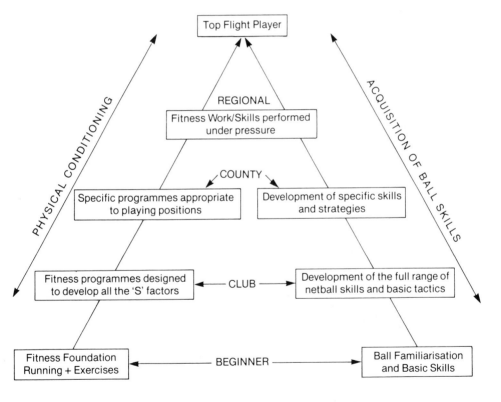

Fig. 130 The development of a player through training

PREPARING AN INDIVIDUAL TRAINING SCHEDULE

Individual differences

The difficulty of designing a team training schedule is that the demands of each position in netball are most specific. This means that a Goal Shooter will require a different programme from a centre-court player. Little research has been done on testing and measuring the actual demands of various positions, but it is obvious that some players cover a great deal of ground whereas others work within a very restricted area. There is equipment which can monitor a player's physical performance during a match and results have reinforced earlier observations. Centre court 'runners' operate at a level which requires aerobic and anaerobic energy, whereas the more 'static' circle players rarely cross the anaerobic threshold. This should not be used as a convenient excuse by the circle players to avoid training! It simply means that their programme needs to take account of this factor and therefore use the training time more purposefully.

There are four ingredients required to make a successful training recipe for any player.

○ knowledge of the fitness 's' factors – strength, speed, suppleness, stamina, skill, psychology
○ knowledge of the training techniques which are available, including weight training, isometric training, power drills (hopping, circuit training, repetition running [shuttle running]), flexibility exercises, popmobility, steady running, fartlek training, skill/endurance circuits
○ knowledge of the particular requirements of a specific playing position
○ knowledge of the individual concerned

TRAINING TECHNIQUES

Circuit training

Circuit training has many advantages for total conditioning. Because of these advantages, leading to aerobic and anaerobic and strength conditioning, circuit training can be recommended as an ideal way of putting all conditioning together during the in-season programme. A circuit specific to netball can be easily utilised by all the players – an example is shown in Table 3. Such a circuit can include muscular endurance, flexibility, and agility exercises as needed by each particular individual.

○ Go through the circuit in Table 3 two or three times without stopping.
○ Work at full speed and take the total time. Then work to improve your time. (Keep a record of your times.)
○ If possible, do the circuit three times a week.

Table 2: *Preparing an individual training schedule*

Fitness factors	Training techniques	Specific requirements e.g. Goal Keeper	Individual analysis
Strength/ power	Weight training, Isometric training, Power drills (hopping, bounding), Skills work against resistance	To spring – leg strength, To control the body in flight, Body strength, To throw accurately – arm strength	Does the player have good spring? Does she get the rebounds? Does she get knocked off balance? Does her throw reach its target?
Speed	Circuit training, Power drills, Repetition running (short shuttle runs)	To manoeuvre quickly in a confined space, Explosive speed (linked with strength), Speed off the mark	Can she move off quickly to left and right? Can she cover a sudden sprint dodge to left or right?
Suppleness/ agility	Flexibility exercises, Popmobility	To extend fully to both sides of the body, To turn quickly in both directions	Can she reach out well to both sides? Does she lose her opponent if she is made to turn?
Stamina	Steady running (2.4km [1½mi] upwards), Fartlek training, Circuit training, Skill/endurance training	To maintain a high level of skill throughout the game, To work hard in short repeated bursts of activity	Does her skill level drop in the latter part of the game? Does she start to make the wrong decisions towards the end of a match? Does she recover quickly after a short intensive spell of activity?
Skill	Covered in chapters 2 and 3	Crucial for all players	General ball skills, Specific GK skills – rebounding
Psychology	Covered in chapter 8	Mental endurance, Persistence vital	Does her concentration wander during the game?

Table 3: *A typical circuit*

	Repetitions	Laps
Trunk curls	10	Initially two,
Squat jumps	8	increasing to
Dorsal raises	8	three as
Press ups	8 or max.	fitness improves
Step ups (bench 45cm [18in] high)	10 each leg leading	
Salmon snaps	10	
Squat thrusts	8	

Weight training

As part of the close and pre-season training, players may adapt to weights through circuits. After four weeks of circuit work the adaptation process should be sufficient to allow for a better utilisation of weights. The schedules to be used could be made up as shown in Table 4.

Table 4: *Weeks 1 – 4 circuit training*

One-leg bench drives × 10 each leg

Press ups × 10

Squat and heave press (with barbell) × 10   × 6

Two-footed bench astride jumps × 10

Sit ups × 10

Chins or dips × 5 or 10

Method

Progress from one exercise to another, then repeat the circuit – and so on.

Week 1: 2 circuits/10 minutes' mobility work
Week 2: 2 circuits/10 minutes' mobility work/1 circuit
Week 3: 2 circuits/10 minutes' mobility work/2 circuits
Week 4: as for Week 3, but with maximum chins/dips; astride jumps

Exercise description

One-leg bench drives: Place one foot on a bench and vigorously extend to produce a vertical jump. Swap feet after prescribed repeats.

Squat and heave press with barbell: Place barbell on the shoulders and perform a controlled back squat followed by a heave press to arms' length overhead.

Two-footed bench astride jumps: Start on one side of a bench and proceed by jumping with both feet together astride the bench.

Mobility work: This should include ankle-flexibility work, and free-standing lunges.

Table 5: *Weeks 5 – 8 and in-season weight training*

It is strongly recommended that before players attempt weight training they should consult an expert to demonstrate correct techniques.

Exercise	Weeks 5 – 8		In-Season	
	Sets	Repeats	Sets	Repeats
Session 1:				
Power clean	3	8	4	4
Split squats	3	6*	4	4*
Front squats	3	8	4	4
Sit ups (knees bent)	3	20†	4	4.5kg (10 lb) × 12
Session 2:				
Power clean	3	8	4	4
Split squats	3	6*	4	4*
Press behind neck‡	3	8	4	4
Upright rowing	3	8	4	4
Side bends (with one dumbell)	3	8*	4	4*

* each side
† with no weight
‡ seated

Bounding

Another method of increasing leg power and spring is to do regular bounding exercises. You will need cotton reels or small boxes to mark where you land. Ensure that this work is carried out on an appropriate surface; i.e., a floor which is flat and even and has some resilience. Start behind a line.

Bounding *continuously* – do not stop in between – bound five times and mark the point where you land (your 'first landing point'). Turn round and bound five times back, and mark your landing. Turn and start from the *original starting point:* do five bounds and mark where you land. Start from your 'first landing point' and bound back: mark where you land. Start from your *original position* and do as before.

Rest until you feel you are ready to work again – try not to make this too long. Repeat three times.

If you can, measure the first five bounds you did and see how you exceed or fall short of this on subsequent attempts – namely on each individual set of bounds – and also how you increase the distance from week to week.

Running

Shuttle running

Choose one of the examples below for your session:

Example 1

O   distance: 15.25m (50ft) – across a court; across a gym
O   number of runs: 5
O   rest period: 30 seconds (gradually reduce as fitness improves)
O   number of repetitions: 5
O   complete recovery and then repeat

Example 2

O   start at A and go through the series shown in Figure 131 twice without stopping
O   rest for 45 seconds
O   repeat
O   rest for 45 seconds
O   repeat

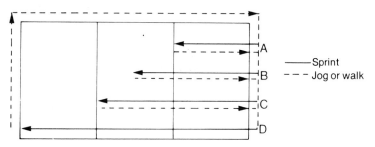

Fig. 131

Example 3

O   repeat the run shown in Figure 132 through three times without rest
O   rest for no longer than one minute
O   repeat three times

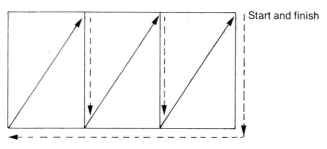

Fig. 132

Cross-country and road running

3 – 8km (2 – 5mi) for 25 – 30 minutes. Run at a steady, even pace.

Fartlek running

Over open country with a variety of surface and slope. A possible schedule is as follows.

- O   easy running: 10 minutes
- O   half pace: 300m (330yd)
- O   walk: 5 minutes
- O   a series of 50m (55yd) sprints interspersed with easy jogging
- O   walk until recovered
- O   fast pace for as long as possible, then jog gently to finish

Interval running

This should be done on an athletics track or football field. Warm up *and* warm down by jogging one complete circuit at the beginning and end of the training. A possible schedule is as follows.

- O   1st circuit: jog 100, stride 20, and so on
- O   2nd circuit: spring 40, jog 40, and so on
- O   3rd circuit: jog
- O   4th circuit: sprint 40, jog 40, and so on
- O   5th circuit: jog
- O   6th circuit: sprint 40, jog 40, and so on

Within-practice conditioning

One technique of aerobic and anaerobic conditioning often overlooked by coaches and players is within-practice conditioning. This term simply suggests that aerobic and anaerobic overload can occur in several ways during skills practice or in actual game practice.

Players should be alert to take advantage of conditioning opportunities within the skills practice session. In netball, for example, when games and practices run continuously with only a short interval of rest, there is overload on the anaerobic system. The player is practising the skills involved in the sport, but she is also producing higher levels of conditioning in the anaerobic system.

Skill and endurance work

Shooters

Example 1

○   record the number of goals scored out of 20 attempts taken from anywhere in the region of the shuttle, as shown in Figure 133. Take a full rest and repeat four times.

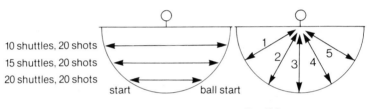

10 shuttles, 20 shots

15 shuttles, 20 shots

20 shuttles, 20 shots

start   ball start

Fig. 133   *Fig. 134*

Example 2

○   4 shuttles moving forward/backwards as shown in Figure 134
○   4 shots
○   4 shuttles moving side to side (bend and touch ground)
○   4 shots
○   keep record of goals scored
○   30 seconds' recovery, then move to line 2 and repeat
○   30 seconds recovery, then move to line 3, and so on through to line 5
○   full recovery and repeat through four times

Defences

Example 1

○   shuttle forward and backwards (in most efficient and appropriate way) as shown in Figure 135, 4 times – 4 leaps to touch the net
○   *using the goal line,* 4 side-to-side shuttles – bend and touch the floor
○   60 seconds' rest, then move to line 2 and repeat
○   at the end of line 5, rest for no more than 5 minutes
○   repeat four times in all

Defences

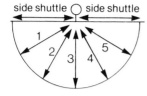

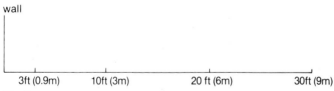

Fig. 135   *Fig. 136*

Example 2

O continuous high balls fed by A (in Figure 136) for 3 minutes
O change over, or take 3 minutes' rest
O repeat twice

Centre court

Example 1

O Jump from 3ft mark (see Figure 137) as if to 'intercept'. Land and sprint to 10ft mark. Touch mark.
O Sprint to 3ft mark and jump to 'intercept'. Land and sprint to 20ft mark. Touch mark.
O Sprint to 3ft mark and jump to 'intercept'. Land and sprint to 30ft mark. Touch mark.
O Sprint to 3ft mark and jump to 'intercept'. Land and sprint to 20ft mark.
O Continue through to 10ft mark and finally 3ft mark.
O Rest for 1½ minutes. Repeat four times.

wall

3ft (0.9m)   10ft (3m)   20 ft (6m)   30ft (9m)

Fig. 137

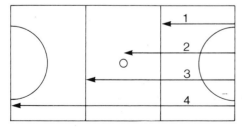

Fig. 138

Example 2

O   Sprint from goal line (see Figure 138) to first-third line. Jump and land on right foot. Pivot round quickly on left foot and jog back.
O   Turn and sprint to centre circle. Jump and land on both feet at once. Pivot and jog back to goal line.
O   Turn and sprint to second-third line. Spring and land on left foot. Pivot on right foot and jog back.
O   Turn and sprint the full length of the court. Jump to touch the goal net.
O   Rest for 1½ minutes and repeat.
O   Rest for 5 minutes, then do the above through again.

Example 3

O   repeat the run shown in Figure 139 five times without rest
O   rest for no longer than three minutes
O   repeat through five times

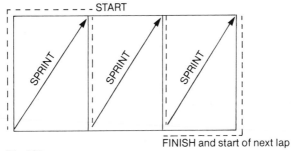

Fig. 139

THE TRAINING YEAR

It is important to structure the programme of the training year by providing divisions of varying duration in the total training. Training should be considered as a cyclical year-long process which is but a part of a total progression of training covering several years. This approach, known as periodisation, is an organised division of the training year in pursuit of basic objectives:

O   to prepare the player for achievement of an optimum improvement in performance
O   to prepare the player for a definite climax to the competitive season
O   to prepare the player for the main competitions associated with that climax
O   to prepare the player for the above objectives in subsequent years by increasing special training status and stabilising technique or performance, over a period of one or more years
O   when appropriate, to aid recovery from injury, illness or a particular stressful training period

In putting the programme together, the divisions used are *preparation, competition* and *transition*; and the framework would be organised as shown in the next few pages.

Off-season (preparation: phase 1)

Most players of a good level recognise the necessity to maintain physical conditioning during the off-season. Maintenance of aerobic and anaerobic conditioning and strength work during the off-season period reduces the chore of particularly hard intensive pre-season training of, often, doubtful value. It is also a particularly important time for overcoming previously exposed limitations and weaknesses.

The off-season period is an ideal time to concentrate on aerobic conditioning for players. Time is available for the continuous type of training: continuous aerobic conditioning, such as running 3km (2mi) at least three times a week, is an effective means of developing a good *aerobic conditioning base* for the player.

Anaerobic conditioning does not receive as much emphasis during the off-season. There are several reasons for this. For most sports there is a gradual increase in the intensity of training from the off-season to the pre-season to the in-season period. Anaerobic conditioning is very intense both physiologically and psychologically. There are real problems of psychological fatigue when intense anaerobic training is carried on for months on end. This form of training requires a great deal of persistence and motivation on the part of the player. Inhibition can be built up in the player if it is carried on year-round.

Since the player is not engaged in regular matches during the off-season, she can afford to undertake a more intensive strength programme. An overall increase in strength is desirable at this time and serves as a basis for strength development.

Pre-season (preparation: phase 2)

The objectives of a year-round conditioning programme are to develop and maintain aerobic conditioning and strength during the off-season, increase the intensity of aerobic conditioning during the pre-season, and peak and maintain the aerobic, anaerobic and strength conditioning during the in-season period. If off-season programmes are used properly, pre-season conditioning can be designed to bring the player to a peak of condition in the briefest possible time.

The main goal of the pre-season strength programme is to prepare the player to meet the strength demands of the sport. Strength must be useable at the specific speed of the sport. An often forgotten aspect of sports performance is that strength must be available repeatedly (muscular endurance) during the game or contest. Also, less time is available for strength training during the pre-season period because of the intense concentration on skills and strategy.

In-season (competition)

Players often abandon serious physical conditioning during the in-season period. The reasons voiced are usually lack of time, the claim that conditioning is unnecessary during the season, and the difficulties of arranging a conditioning programme in terms of facilities and equipment. *Physical condition and strength increases are reversible.* The athlete who trains seriously and diligently in the pre-season period faces the prospect that a certain amount of deconditioning may take place during the season.

Aerobic conditioning can be maintained with as little as two or three training sessions of fifteen to thirty minutes per week. Obviously the minimum time period would not suffice for highly aerobic sports, but it should maintain 'base aerobic conditioning' for most netball players. A combination warm-up run and aerobic-conditioning period prior to practice will meet the requirements set forth for maintaining aerobic conditioning. Anaerobic conditioning can be maintained by essentially the same interval-training techniques used in the pre-conditioning period.

The main goals of in-season strength training are to maintain the strength level demanded of the sport and to help prevent injuries. Like aerobic conditioning, strength and power can be maintained by far less work than is required to attain peak levels of strength and power.

To aid in injury prevention, the areas of the body most subject to injury should be given special attention. Maintaining strength in those muscle groups will reduce the risk of muscle injury. A sample training schedule is shown in Table 6.

Table 6: *Training schedule*

Saturday	Club/County match
Sunday	1½/2 mile run (varying speed); mobility exercises; circuit training
Monday	Ball handling skills; shuttle and bounds
Tuesday	Club/County practice; circuit training
Wednesday	Ball handling skills; 1½/2 miles run (steady run)
Thursday	Skill and endurance circuit; shuttle running
Friday	REST DAY

Note: It is always better to do skill work before endurance or strength training whenever possible.

OTHER CONSIDERATIONS

Warm up and warm down

There have been some conflicting opinions about the type and extent of warm up required before a training session or match. There is little doubt that a well structured routine which involves a general 'awakening' of body and mind does enhance performance (see Figure 140). Evidence suggests that if a

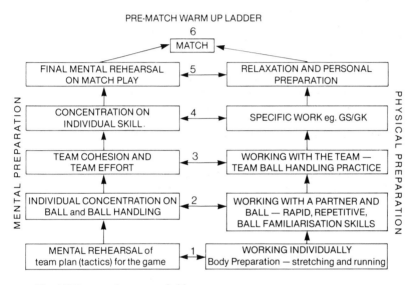

PRE-MATCH WARM UP LADDER

Fig. 140 Pre-match warm up ladder

muscle is warmed the speed with which it contracts and relaxes and the force of contraction are increased. When an inactive muscle is called into action, there is a local rise in temperature and an accumulation of metabolic products. This results in an increase in local blood flow through the muscle which in turn increases the oxygen supply and consequently improves the functional condition of the muscle.

A warm up can also provide mental stimulation and an opportunity to rehearse skills both physically and mentally. It is a time for the team to gain confidence, composure and cohesion before the match begins.

As with the training programme, the same factors must be brought into consideration when designing a warm-up schedule. There should be a progressive build-up of physical effort accompanied by a gradual increase in skill level and a narrowing of the focus of attention.

All athletes, including netball players, should include a brief after-match or after-training warm down. This usually takes the form of a relaxed jogging session. It helps the player to 'unwind' physically and mentally and may help prevent some stiffness and injury.

Exercise and heat and temperature regulations

Heat magnifies normal responses to work and consequently players performing in hot environments may show signs of undue stress. In a warm climate stress can be created because body heat is more difficult to dissipate.

Women have a larger number of active sweat glands than men, but do not begin to sweat until the temperature is 2 – 3 Centigrade degrees higher than men. That their sweating threshold is higher may be due to the inhibitory effect of oestrogen. It has been found that when oestrogen levels are low – during the early stages of menstruation – women begin to sweat at lower temperature. Generally women manage to regulate their body temperature efficiently by adjusting their sweat rate to the required heat loss.

Due to good insulation (10% more adipose tissue in females than males) the skin temperature is high and this makes individuals feel warm. This may lead players to believe that the pre-activity warm up is not necessary, but that is a totally false assumption. Coaches and players need to be aware of the possible extra strain which may occur in a hot climate and adjust their programmes accordingly.

The ability to work in hot/dry or hot/humid environments depends largely upon a water intake that is sufficient to replace the water lost in sweat. The body will not retain water unless there is a salt to go with it. If a salt deficit is accumulated, the player may suffer from dehydration, nausea and cramp – and in extreme cases may collapse. Salt given without water produces gastro-intestinal discomfort, but given with water it brings about an improvement in heat tolerance. Water and salt should be given in small and frequent (hourly) amounts in hot climates. In some circumstances slow sodium may be used as an alternative to salt.

It is also important to maintain an adequate intake of carbohydrates, total calories and water-soluble vitamins. Replacement of vitamins and minerals lost through sweating is essential for efficient performance in humid heat.

Sport and the menstrual cycle

Concern is often expressed that sport interferes with the normal menstrual cycle, but there are no medical reasons why women should not take part in netball at all phases of the cycle. There may be some small fluctuation in an individual's level of performance: while women have achieved record-breaking and match-winning performances at all stages of the menstrual cycle, many do report a 'falling off' of performance. The evidence is presently so ambivalent that one can only conclude that each individual player needs to make a personal assessment of the variability and adjust their play or training accordingly.

Research evidence suggests that a high level of fitness and regular exercise may lead to a reduction in period pains, although other side-effects – premenstrual discomfort, fluid retention – are apparently unchanged. Exposure to very intensive training stress may induce menstrual problems, which will in turn affect performance levels.

It is equally true that, if blood loss is consistently greater than average, anaemia may develop. This is a debilitating disorder which may reduce a player's effectiveness and require medical attention.

Amenorrhoea (absence of periods) is seen in some distance runners who cover very high mileages. Secondary amenorrhoea can result from excessive weight loss, but generally the type of training undertaken by netball players should not produce this condition.

For most players, training and match play may go on with little or no regard to the menstrual cycle, while others may need to take account of performance variations, remembering that these could be psychological rather than physiological in origin.

CONCLUSION

It is essential to develop the right attitude to training and preparation for performance: the right 'training habits'. There is a need for the player to consider the various factors and aspects of conditioning outlined, and to prepare an organised, progressive and relevant schedule using a cyclical year-round approach which produces the desired effects and the achievement of optimum performance when it is required. Although many factors contribute to success in any sport, there is no doubt about the significant contribution of sound, organised preparation to effective performance.

Chapter 8

The contribution of sports psychology to netball

Jim Golby

Jim Golby, M.A., *is a senior lecturer in human movement studies at Leeds Polytechnic. He trained as a physical education teacher, and completed an Advanced Diploma at Carnegie and a Master's Degree at Leeds University. His interests are in the psychology of skilled behaviour; his research interests include the measurement of skilled performance and the effects of psychotropic drugs on perceptual motor skill.*

It is necessary to limit the content of an introductory chapter on the psychology of netball to areas of immediate relevance and value. Figure 141 outlines some of the major areas of psychological enquiry which shed understanding on the coaching of netball and illustrates the vast area from which selection has been made. Such a selection involves a value judgement which is invidious. It is hoped that coaches might use the following findings as a springboard to further reading and study and as a means of introduction to the rapidly developing field of sports psychology.

SKILL VARIABLES

Netball involves many skills which are never perfected. The player is always at some stage of learning; sometimes at an advanced stage, but always learning. This is especially true of skills which are performed in a changing environment where players move about, where the path and speed of the ball constantly alter, and where playing conditions frequently differ. It is, nevertheless, possible to make significant improvements, and appropriate *practice* helps maintain and improve the level of skill. Conversely, absence of practice, or poorly constructed practice schedules, lead to a regression in the level of performance.

Feedback

Feedback represents the dynamic interaction between practice and performance. The coach helps, by feedback, to draw attention to the relationship between particular kinds of action and the results of those actions. Performance has been shown to improve more rapidly when more detailed feedback is given.

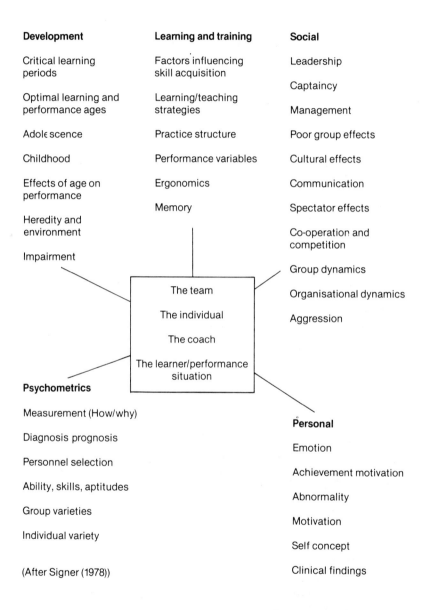

Development

Critical learning periods

Optimal learning and performance ages

Adolescence

Childhood

Effects of age on performance

Heredity and environment

Impairment

Learning and training

Factors influencing skill acquisition

Learning/teaching strategies

Practice structure

Performance variables

Ergonomics

Memory

Social

Leadership

Captaincy

Management

Poor group effects

Cultural effects

Communication

Spectator effects

Co-operation and competition

Group dynamics

Organisational dynamics

Aggression

The team

The individual

The coach

The learner/performance situation

Psychometrics

Measurement (How/why)

Diagnosis prognosis

Personnel selection

Ability, skills, aptitudes

Group varieties

Individual variety

(After Signer (1978))

Personal

Emotion

Achievement motivation

Abnormality

Motivation

Self concept

Clinical findings

Fig. 141 Areas of psychological enquiry which have relevance to the coaching of netball

Feedback can play three important roles in coaching. Firstly it can act as a source of motivation; secondly, as reinforcement; or, thirdly, to regulate behaviour.

It should be borne in mind that the players, even while performing, are obtaining some kind of internal feedback; that is to say, they are gaining the feel of the movement. The coach has gradually to ensure that the player develops the ability to distinguish between the correct and the incorrect movement pattern by drawing attention to inappropriate aspects of the movement and showing how these lead to inappropriate outcomes.

A summary of the effects of feedback suggests that learning is a function of the quality of the feedback given. There is a gradual decline in performance with a delay in feedback and an even greater decline when feedback is withheld. It seems, then, that feedback is instrumental in learning, and that, the better the quality of feedback (e.g., augmented feedback – such as when comparing a performance with an ideal model, offering coaching loops, films or international players for comparison), the more rapid and complete the learning.

Guidance

Skills learning is made easier by sound guidance given by an informed coach. Guidance refers to a large variety of separate procedures and techniques, but the three most often used in coaching are

O   visual
O   verbal
O   physical

Guidance procedures are intended to prevent the learner from making errors in the tasks and to speed up the learning of the correct technique. The visual guidance most often used is the demonstration (see chapter 5).

Verbal guidance

Verbal guidance is the use of voice (much loved by the majority of coaches). It comes as a shock that the voice is a relatively ineffective means of guidance, especially when preparing to work at an advanced level on skills which are complex. In some cases, however, the voice is the only means of giving insight into some of the nuances of play, but this is best done during rest periods and, where possible, kept to an absolute minimum.

Physical guidance

Physical guidance in terms of netball means putting the player's body through the required movements so that the player can experience the feel of the movement. This form of guidance, 'forced response', is often useful but – a word of warning – there is some evidence to suggest that such guidance can give the wrong feeling for the skill being taught. Another and perhaps superior kind of guidance is termed 'restriction', and occurs where the player is relatively free to move, but certain unwanted or harmful movements are blocked out. This is a less oppressive and intimidating method than forced response. Both techniques have been found to be effective in teaching various skills but need careful monitoring.

Other variables

Fatigue is a factor which impairs both the learning and the performance of netball skills. Where possible, especially in the younger player, the effects of fatigue must be carefully monitored, even to the extent of scaling down the size of the equipment used and the length of playing and practice sessions.

Another important factor which interferes with learning and consequently impairs performance is mental: the coach attempting to teach too much too soon. In other words, she *overloads* the player. It must be borne in mind that material which has been taught and partly learned needs a chance to settle in the mind of the player before the coach tries to push anything else in on top of it. If this is not done, the coach will find either that the two skills have become confused or that the learning of one subject has wiped out the recall of the other.

Skill can be seen to involve three related components. Firstly, *perception*; i.e., how the player reads and understands the many cues which present themselves during a game. Secondly, *decision-making*, which includes how the player matches the cues received to the recall of the past experiences and the present state of the play, and then decides upon an appropriate course of action. Thirdly, *response*, the way in which the selected action is carried out. The implications of such a breakdown of any skill to the coach are

O   it is possible to better understand the tasks of teaching (which is the introduction of novel material) and of coaching (which is the improvement of skills partly learned), in a much more detailed and informed way
O   it is much easier to locate and correct failures in performance
O   it enables a more logical, appropriate and economical use of practice time

MOTIVATIONAL VARIABLES

Psychology has long since indicated that players do not necessarily perform all skills most efficiently when arousal is extremely high. An individual player must be aroused to a level above her normal resting state but not too highly. The level of arousal sought by the coach, and the means used to acquire it, depend upon such factors as the personality of the individual player, the nature of the task or skill to be performed, and the state of learning of the player on that particular skill.

All people are aroused to a greater or a lesser extent. They shift along a continuum as they experience the different happenings of the day. They vary from deep sleep to a state of high excitement (it should be pointed out that the state of high excitement might well be identified as stress, anxiety, emotion, drive or even motivation). What adds interest to this idea is the fact that one player, let us say Jean, normally varies between points (i) and (ii) on the continuum shown in Figure 142, whereas Anne normally varies between points (iii) and (iv). Jean and Anne represent typical types of players.

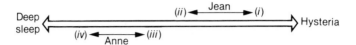

Fig. 142 Individual differences in everyday levels of arousal

Jean might be described as 'extraverted' and Anne as 'introverted'. It is obvious that some players, such as Jean, are sociable, outgoing and often are aroused by interaction with other people. She tends to be in control of her emotions and does not lose her temper very quickly. Such a person usually does well on the big occasions, but is a little loath to practise and train alone, and needs more motivating at ordinary coaching sessions and more correction in tasks of a repetitive or simple nature.

By contrast, Anne is less happy when in the company of other people – indeed, seems to avoid it at times – and does not see other players as a source of motivation or arousal. She has a quick temper and is very sensitive to criticism.

Such personalities as Anne and Jean are clearly stereotypes, but they serve to exemplify how different players need handling in a different fashion if the coach is to help them to obtain their best level of learning and performance. The coach needs to ensure each player is in her optimum state for the task in hand. The more demanding or complex the task – e.g., initially learning footwork ot learning a new type of response under pressure – the lower the motivational state or level of arousal which should be sought.

Some occasions or activities will, of themselves, arouse the player; e.g., a cup final, a play-off, final regional trials, representative squad sessions. Such arousal may well be ideal for one player but may prove too much for another. The problem is further complicated by the difficulty of assessing the level of arousal. External appearance is not always the best indicator since introverts tend to mask their inner feelings rather well and extraverts tend to exaggerate theirs. The most sensitive and accurate means available to the coach for such an assessment are not within the scope of this chapter; suffice it to say that, once alerted to such differences and the problems they pose, the more perceptive coach can quickly evolve her own strategies based on careful observation and experience.

Evidence tends to suggest that, once a skill has been developed to a high level and is well learned, a high level of motivation is required for optimum performance. Conversely skills which are either novel, or demanding, or provide a challenge, or offer an incentive tend to raise the level of arousal and thus require a lower initial starting level.

Coaches will therefore need to seek techniques which enable them to change the state of arousal in any desired direction. Some such techniques may well be already familiar to them. For instance, arousal can be raised by altering such variables as competition (challenge), praise and blame/reproof, reward and punishment, the pep talk, music and, of increasing popularity, biofeedback. It is an irony that some of the above techniques have been used also to lower arousal levels; for example, soft and soothing music may well help to calm a player prior to a big game.

In summary, it is useful to offer these generalisations which derive directly from empirical psychological research.

O   a higher level of arousal is essential for optimum performance in aspects of netball which involve gross motor activity and include power and endurance

O   a high level of arousal interferes with performances involving complex skill, fine coordination, steadiness and concentration

O   a slightly above normal level of arousal is preferable to a subnormal or normal level of arousal for the learning and performance of netball skills

O   individuals differ in their basal levels of arousal and consequently need differential handling by coaches in order to ensure optimum learning and performance

O   outward appearance is a poor indicator of inner states

SOCIAL VARIABLES

It is clear that the course of our lives is irrevocably affected and influenced by our experiences with others. This is true in private relationships, in small group encounters and in the larger bodies and organisations which make up society. The study of social psychology is chiefly concerned with the understanding of the nature of these interactions and relationships. The game of netball is a ripe area from which to apply the findings of social psychology.

One of the important areas of study within the field of social psychology is how the presence of others affects our performance. It will be clear that the presence of others can occur in a number of forms. The two most frequently encountered are, firstly, in the form of an audience and, secondly, in the form of a fellow performer or co-actor. The former is an obvious topic of interest to the coach, who will want to know what effect the presence of spectators has upon the learning or performance of netball skill.

Research findings suggest that, when a task is not very well learned or is very difficult, the vast number of incorrect responses are dominant and in this case the correct response is weak. The presence of others results in a disruption of performance. By contrast, when a task is well learned or is extremely simple, the correct response is the dominant one and incorrect responses are very weak. In this case the presence of others results in a significant performance improvement.

An important consideration for the coach is the type of atmosphere she should attempt to create in which the players will learn and perform. This may well be seen in terms of *group cohesion*, which can be defined as the total field of forces causing members to remain in the group or, conversely, resist disruption. Whatever the definition, it is the adhesive property of the group, the force that binds it together, that needs to be considered.

A conclusion that is repeatedly demonstrated in research is that there are many different types and kinds of cohesion. For example, the coach may engender cohesion by selecting a team whose members enjoy each other's company. Another way of engendering cohesion is to place membership to the coach's group on a high pedestal; that is to say, make membership highly prestigious, the group very select. This often tends to produce feelings of solidarity, unity and togetherness. Another type of cohesion is that brought about by well drilled, smooth-running team play. The important factor for the coach is that she is aware that cohesiveness can be engendered by a number of ways and that it is very important in the construction of a successful team.

One way of ensuring that the correct group atmosphere is created is to realise the importance and strength of the phenomenon of *social reinforcement*. Most people – even if they have only a superficial grasp of the work of the early psychologists – are aware that behaviour which is rewarded or reinforced tends to be strengthened and behaviour which is not reinforced is weakened. It would appear that social reinforcement is an effective source of information to the player, as well as being a motivator. Indeed, of all the possible behaviour strategies offered by the coach, the ones which have the greatest consequences or impact upon players involve social-reinforcement: praise, gestures, smiles, criticism, reproof and so on.

The coach who is aware of this social psychological perspective will examine the situational causes of behaviour and the way in which the individual player perceives these factors. This perspective will give her valuable aid in understanding the processes of social influence which can help her structure coaching sessions and select appropriate team leaders. It will also give insights into such aspects as the relationship between cooperation and competition, poor group effects, cultural effects and the communications network within a squad of players.

PERSONALITY VARIABLES

'Personality' refers to the individual's whole psychological make-up. It includes such aspects as temperament, character, intelligence, sentiments, beliefs, attitudes, ideals, values and interests. The personality of a person is shown by their dispositions and by the way in which these dispositions are organised. The development of personality is partly due to inherited characteristics and partly due to experience and upbringing.

The study of personality is the most frequently reported topic in sports psychology. It should be noted that it is also one of the most contentious, since there exist at least sixty definitions of the term. It is hardly surprising that a number of problems are associated with its exact description and measurement.

However, an approach suggested by Eysenck might well give the coach some insight into the way in which a knowledge of personality can help in understanding individual players. For Eysenck, personality differs along two dimensions, namely extraversion/introversion and neuroticism/stability.

In terms of behaviour, the typical extravert is sociable, craves change and excitement, acts impulsively and takes risks. The typical introvert is a quiet, withdrawn and introspective person, who tends to be of a serious disposition with a well ordered mode of life.

These differences in personality seem to indicate the superiority of the extravert in terms of suitability for netball. But this is not always the case, since skills which require vigilance (close marking) or contain long periods of sustained repetitive effort (shooting) will suit the introvert better.

Although the dimension of extraversion/introversion has attracted most interest, the dimension of neuroticism/stability cannot be ignored. At one end of this continuum we have people whose emotions are strong and easily aroused: they tend to be moody, touchy and restless. At the other extreme are people who are calm, even-tempered, reliable and carefree. The former are described as neurotics, the latter as stable. The implications of such a classification for the coach need no explanation.

In order to give any meaning to a classification of personality such as the one described, it is essential to be able to measure these characteristics of such a classification which are exhibited by the person. This takes us into the realm of psychometrics, or psychological measurement. To be able to measure and to understand the meanings, implications and limitations of the results obtained would take much more detailed information than this chapter of the book can hope to provide: the chapter's introduction stressed the developing nature of psychology. Consequently, there is not, as yet, any one theory of personality which connects all aspects. Any adequate account of personality must embrace at least three perspectives: (a) the situation determinants, (b) personality variables and (c) how the person views the experience. Eysenck's work places greatest emphasis on the personality variables and thus gives only part of the answer. There exist many different theories of personality which give some insight into individual make-up; many of these theories involve some type of measurement. The field of psychology is therefore rich in information of potential value to the coach. Only a more thorough and detailed study would allow the coach to derive maximum benefit from such knowledge and permit meaningful use of many of the forms of assessment now available.

CONCLUSION

This chapter has set out to achieve a number of objectives. It has attempted to justify the study of psychology as a worthwhile enterprise for the coach, and attempted to identify and explain some of the major areas of relevance which have been scientifically examined by psychologists. Secondly, it has attempted to outline some of the implications of such research for the coach, especially in terms of the planning and structure of coaching sessions. In doing so, it has hopefully achieved another objective by sensitising the coach to the emergent field of sports psychology and motivating her to explore this important area of knowledge at a much deeper level.

Chapter 9

Diet and nutrition

Wilf Paish

Wilf Paish *was appointed as a national athletics coach in 1964, and has been involved in that occupation ever since. He has been a team coach at the Olympic Games, Commonwealth Games and European Championships. He has travelled widely and mixed with sportsmen and -women, trainers, coaches and sports scientists from all over the world, and in many instances acted as their adviser. He has a particular interest in diet in sport and has lectured on this subject at international symposia. He has also written extensively on this as well as most other aspects of sports science.*

THE ENERGY BALANCE

For perfect balance, the Caloric equivalent of the food ingested should equal that of the energy expended in supporting life and activity. Should it swing in the favour of the food intake then the extra Calories are deposited about the body in the form of fat. Should there be a negative balance, then the body will start to use up its protein stores for energy, which places the body in a *katabolic* (breaking-down) process, the ultimate effect of which is death.

The average woman has an energy expenditure of, probably, about 2,000Cal. Those actively involved in netball and other sports are likely to expend in excess of 4,000Cal; i.e., about twice the average.

The first step in the assessment of the daily energy expenditure is to calculate the basal rate. This is the energy required to support twenty-four hours of bed rest (Table 7). It varies with weight, height, sex and age. To this basal rate should be added the energy costs of daily chores (Table 8), and the energy costs for the particular sport (Table 9). Hence energy requirements = basal + chores + sport. Approximations can be made as follows:

Activity	% above basal
Quiet sitting	30
Light activity (office work)	50
Moderate activity (housework)	70
Heavy occupation (manual work/sport)	100

Table 7: *For calculating the basal rate (24 hours' bed rest)*

WOMEN

Weight		*Approx. Caloric expenditure*
lb	kg	
100	45	1,225
120	54	1,320
140	64	1,400
160	73	1,485
180	82	1,575

These calculations are based on the female norm of 1.68m (5ft 6in), and an age of 25 years.

Table 8: *A few selected examples of the effect of daily chores upon the total Caloric expenditure*

Activity	*Calories/kg/hour*
Sleep	0.93
Resting – not asleep	1.10
Sitting still	1.43
Free standing	1.50
Class work	1.70
Fast typing	2.00
Slow walking	2.86
Carrying bag (50kg)	6.52
Walking upstairs	6.00
House work	5.70
Dressing/undressing	1.69

Should a person wish to calculate precisely the energy expended in a day then a careful log of each activity and its duration must be recorded. For example, for the 64kg (140 lb) player, just washing/dressing in the morning (including making up) is likely to take about 15min. Therefore the approximate recording for this everyday chore is

$$\underset{\text{(energy cost)}}{1.69} \times \underset{\text{(weight in kilos)}}{64} \div \underset{(\frac{1}{4}\text{hr})}{4} = \underset{\text{(total)}}{2.644\text{Cal}}$$

Table 9: *The energy costs of activities associated with sport*

Activity	Approx. Calories/kg/hr
Netball	7.00
Running slow (15km/hr)	11.25
Running fast (400m/min)	85.00
Calisthenics	6.50
Jumping/bounding	15.00
Weight training	20.00
Swimming (recreational)	12.00
Badminton	8.00
Tennis	10.00

Table 10: *This illustrates a typical example of an international woman netball player. I have chosen the activities which I think a good netballer should include in a training scheme.*

Details: age – 25 years, height – 1.68m (5ft 6in), weight – 60kg (9st 7lb), occupation – physical education teacher

Basal	= 1,400
Chores + work = 100%	= 1,400
Basic cost without sport	= 2,800

Day with a game of 1 hour

Basal	= 2,800
Game	= 540
Total	= 3,340

Day with training*

Basal	= 2,800
10min jog	= 112
10 × 100m sprints	= 360
10min calisthenics	= 90
1hr skill training	= 540
Total	= 3,902

If one adds to this the acts of walking up/down stairs, walking to catch the bus, standing in the bus queue, typing, etc., then a number of small units add up to something quite large and significant.

The approximate energy costs for the player described in Table 10 will be in the region of 3,902, which supports my earlier hypothesis of it being about twice that for the average person not involved in sport. In view of this, the netball player will need to eat about twice as much as the average woman in order to satisfy the demands for energy. However, as will be emphasised several times in this chapter, the monitoring of basal body weight (the weight recorded early in the morning with an empty bladder) will give a sound indication as to whether the balance is correct.

THE NETBALLER'S BASIC DEMAND FOR FOODSTUFFS

The basic diet requirements are proteins, carbohydrates, fats, vitamins, minerals, liquids and roughage. Participation in sport disturbs homoeostasis (the chemical balance of the body), and there is a need for it to return back to normal as quickly as possible. Nutrition plays an important role in this respect.

Proteins

Of the three basic nutrients, protein is the only one essential to the body: it is required by the body for a number of reasons. The cells of the body are composed of protein and they are constantly undergoing change, being broken down in the general 'wear and tear' of life. The cells require proteins for the rebuilding process, and probably the most significant point in this area is related to muscle protein. The act of training and participation calls for the muscle protein to be broken down; the process of rebuilding the muscle, to make it stronger than its original state, is a result of the intricate action of proteins and hormones.

Proteins also contribute to the enzyme pool, so making the chemical process of life more efficient. They have a marked effect upon certain hormones which again contribute significantly to the efficiency of life.

Another very important function of protein is the role it plays in the delicate nitrogen balance. It is the body's only source of nitrogen. Research indicates that the nitrogen balance is best maintained when the protein ingested is of animal, rather than vegetable, derivation.

Netballers must be fit and aware, capable of making split-second decisions; hence a lower than average protein intake would not be acceptable and could reduce efficiency. While protein is not a main source of direct energy, about 18% of the total energy requirements of a netballer should probably come in the form of protein.

It is not easy for the average person to discover the best sources of protein. In 1956 the United Nations Committee for Food and Agriculture rated the most common sources of protein in rank order. Eggs were found to contain the best balance of essential amino acids and were given the 100% rating. (This does *not* mean that an egg is composed entirely of protein: it is just the percentage given to it in order to place all of the other foods in rank order.) The chart is as follows.

- O   eggs   100%
- O   fish/meat   70%
- O   soya beans   69%
- O   milk   60%
- O   rice   56%
- O   corn   41%

Carbohydrates

These are not essential to the body at all: they are just the most convenient source of energy. The reason for this is that the body can manufacture carbohydrate from both protein and fat.

The netballer requires about 50% of her total energy demand in the form of carbohydrate, which represents about 10g/kg bodyweight. One should guard against sudden large ingestions of sugar, as can be found in glucose drinks and tablets when taken in excess. Here the insulin reaction is triggered off, and this has the effect of reducing blood-sugar levels. In very hot weather carbohydrates should supply about 60% of the energy requirements.

Table 11: *Foods rich in carbohydrates*

Food	g carbohydrate per 100g food
rice	86.8
cornflakes	85.4
honey	76.4
jam	69.2
bread (white)	54.3
bread (brown)	48.3
chips	37.3
potatoes (boiled)	19.7
bananas	19.2
apples	12.0

Fats

These are technically termed lipids and are by many people ignored in sport. They contain a massive store of energy but are wasteful in their use of oxygen. In terms of energy production, they release about twice as much as do carbohydrates – although, when the body is working at almost full capacity, it is forced to revert to the carbohydrate source.

Fats, which can have a vegetable or an animal source, are essential to the body as they bind the fat-soluble vitamins and have a cosmetic as well as an insulating function.

The total amount of fats necessary for healthy, active life should be approximately the same as for protein – i.e., in the region of 20% of the overall energy requirements.

Table 12: *Foods rich in fats*

Food	g fats per 100g food
margarine	81.5
butter	81.0
nuts	53.5
bacon	40.5
cheese	34.5
lamb	30.2
pork	29.6
eggs	10.9

Vitamins

As far as the woman involved in sport is concerned it is almost certain that there will not be a shortfall in the nutrients that provide energy. The simple bodyweight tests would soon establish this. However, the same thing could not be said with any degree of certainty in respect of vitamins.

Although the study of vitamins has been in progress now for about a century, few people know precisely what they are or what they do. A fairly safe and simple idea is to regard vitamins as the catalysts of nutritional chemistry. That is, they speed up or make more efficient the chemical processes involved in getting the nutrients from the food which we eat.

Vitamins are divided into two basic classifications: there are those which are fat-soluble, namely vitamins A, D, E and K; and the water-soluble vitamins of the B and C groups.

Vitamin A

Vitamin A can be taken directly into the body through one of the fish liver oils or indirectly *via* the carotene in vegetables and fruit. Tables 13 and 14 on the following pages will give an indication of the foods containing vitamin A and, as long as some of these are included in the diet, supplementation should not be necessary.

Table 13: *Composition of foods per 100g*

							Vitamins					
Food	Protein g	Fat g	Carbohydrate g	Water g	Calcium mg	Iron mg	A µg	B₁ mg	B₂ mg	B₃ mg	C mg	D µg
Beef	18.1	17.1		64	7	1.9	0	0.06	0.19	8.1	0	0
Lamb	15.9	30.2		53	7	1.3	0	0.09	0.19	7.4	0	0
Pork	15.8	29.6		54	8	0.8	0	0.58	0.16	6.9	0	0
Chicken	20.8	6.7		73	11	1.5	0	0.04	0.17	9.5	0	0
Liver	20.7	8.0	2.2	69	6	11.4	6,000	0.26	3.10	18.1	30	0.75
Bacon	14.4	40.5	0	41	7	1.0	0	0.36	0.14	5.8	0	0
Sausages (beef)	9.6	24.1	11.7	50	48	1.4	0	0.03	0.13	7.1	0	0
Fish	17.4	0.7	0	82	16	0.3	0	0.08	0.07	4.8	0	0
Eggs	12.3	10.9	0	75	54	2.1	140	0.09	0.47	3.7	0	1.5
Milk	3.3	3.8	4.8	88	120	0.1	44	0.04	0.15	0.9	1	0.05
Cheese	25.4	34.5	0	37	810	0.6	420	0.04	0.50	5.2	0	0.35
Butter	0.5	81.0	0	16	15	0.2	995	0	0	0.1	0	1.25
Margarine	0.2	81.5	0	15	4	0.3	900	0	0	0.1	0	8.00
Jam	0.5	0	69.2	30	18	12	2	0	0	0	10	0
Honey	0.4	0	76.4	23	50	0.4	0	0	0.05	0.2	0	0
Beans (runner)	2.2	0	3.9	89	27	0.8	50	0.05	0.10	1.4	20	0
Cabbage	2.8	0	2.8	88	57	0.6	50	0.06	0.05	0.7	53	0
Carrots	0.7	0	5.4	90	48	0.6	2,000	0.06	0.05	0.7	6	0
Peas	5.8	0	10.6	84	15	1.9	50	0.32	0.15	3.5	25	0
Potatoes (chips)	3.8	9	37.3	48	14	1.4	0	0.10	0.04	2.2	6	0
Potatoes (boiled)	1.4	0	19.7	81	4	0.5	0	0.08	0.03	1.2	6	0
Apples	0.3	0	12.0	84	4	0.3	5	0.04	0.02	0.1	5	0
Bananas	1.1	0	19.2	71	7	0.4	33	0.04	0.07	0.8	10	0
Oranges	0.8	0	8.5	86	41	0.3	8	0.10	0.03	0.3	50	0
Nuts (almonds)	20.5	53.5	4.3	5	247	4.2	0	0.32	0.25	4.9	0	0
Bread (white)	8.0	1.7	54.3	39	100	1.7	0	0.18	0.03	2.6	0	0
Bread (brown)	9.2	1.4	48.3	39	88	2.5	0	0.28	0.07	2.7	0	0
Cornflakes	7.4	0.4	85.4	2	5	0.3	0	1.13	1.41	10.6	0	0
Rice	6.2	1.0	86.8	12	4	0.4	0	0.08	0.03	1.5	0	0
Instant Coffee	4	0.7	35.5	2	140	4.0	0	0	0.10	45.7	0	0
Tea	0	0	0	0	0	0	0	0	0	0.9	6	0

Table 14: *Percentage vitamin contributions made by important foods in the average British diet*

Food Group	Vitamins A	B₁	B₂	B₃	C	D
Milk, cheese, eggs	23	17	51	4	9	26
Meat/fish	22	25	21	40	1	26
Cereals (bread, etc.)	2	32	7	28	1	3
Fruit/vegetables	27	25	13	21	87	—
Fats (butter, etc.)	26	1	1	1	—	43
Sugars/preserves	—	—	1	1	1	—

Vitamin B group

This is a complex of vitamins all related to one another in certain ways. Vitamins in this group are soluble in water, and hence they cannot be stored in the body. A daily intake is therefore essential.

Thiamine: vitamin B₁: Like most of the B complex, this is present in wheatgerm oil – that is, the oil found naturally in the wheat-grain kernel. However, it is one of those many vitamins that is almost totally destroyed by the refining process, something which happens to most of our flour. Tables 13, 14 and 15 will give an indication of the amount required and its possible source.

Riboflavin: vitamin B₂: Originally called 'vitamin G', this vitamin is very similar to B₁, having a similar action in muscle chemistry, and is found in the same substances. Tables 13, 14, and 15 give the sources and amounts required.

Niacin: vitamin B₃: This vitamin is also known as nicotinic acid. It is present in yeast and its products, in nuts, fish and meat. It is a vital vitamin in the production of energy, in that it helps to form an enzyme which aids the assimilation of carbohydrates, and is a necessary catalyst for the functioning of vitamins B₁ and B₂.

Pyridoxine: vitamin B₆: The most important role of this complicated vitamin is in the metabolism of proteins. Like most of the B group, it is present in the unrefined wheat grain and to a lesser extent in meat, poultry, fish and vegetables, the latter being our greatest source.

Pantothenic acid: Again this vitamin plays an important part in the production of energy from our basic foodstuffs.

Biotin: This is an essential vitamin in the metabolism of fats and the subsequent release of energy for fuelling our muscular activity.

Vitamin B₁₂: This is the one member of the vitamin B group not found in yeast products. However, both meat and dairy products have a high yield, and the only person likely to suffer a deficiency is the true vegetarian. It is important in the development of cells, most notably blood cells. Because the red blood cell is the oxygen-carrying pigment of the blood, any person involved with sport cannot afford to be low on this vitamin. As women involved in competitive sport are prone to anaemia, it is more important for them to take the necessary precautions by eating the correct foods.

The body requires about 5μm of B_{12} per day and, as a normal diet containing both meat and dairy products will provide easily twice this amount, there is little need for supplementation.

Folic acid: This is a vitamin which works in conjunction with vitamin B_{12}, and has a very important function in the prevention of anaemia. The body requires about 400μg of this vitamin each day. Its dietary sources are deep green leafy vegetables, root vegetables and lean meat. If these are present in the diet a deficiency of this vitamin is unlikely.

In conclusion to this section on the vitamin B group, the group's importance in sport and in particular for women should be reemphasised. While I do not recommend indiscriminate supplementation, this is one group where, because it is water-soluble and so not toxic, the added insurance of supplementation against a deficiency is worthwhile. A daily intake of brewer's yeast tablets, which are very inexpensive, and a few slices of wholemeal bread are all that is required.

Vitamin C: ascorbic acid

This is certainly the vitamin about which the majority of people have the most knowledge. Vitamin C has wide and complicated effects upon the body. It is involved in, for example,

O   the formation of intercellular collagens found in fibrous tissue, bone, cartilage, etc.
O   the formation of the amino acids involved in the production of collagens which aid wound-healing and the ability to withstand the stress of injury and infection
O   cellular respiration
O   the absorption of iron, an essential pigment for the transportation of oxygen and hydrogen
O   the correct functioning of the adrenal glands

From this shortened list it can be seen that vitamin C can have a most significant effect upon performance in sport.

The vitamin is available in most fresh fruit and vegetables, as Table 13 illustrates. But it must be pointed out that cooking almost completely destroys the vitamin and that storing, preserving and refrigeration considerably reduce its presence.

There are other vitamins, such as vitamin D (calciferol), vitamin E (tocopherol), vitamin K and vitamin P, but the total study of vitamins is beyond the scope of this chapter, which is concerned to give a basic understanding of those most likely to affect the performance of a netball player.

Minerals

Most people believe that minerals and vitamins are the same, but this is far from correct. While their effects upon the body might be similar, their actions are entirely different.

Basically, the minerals acting on the body form two quite distinct groups: those essential for the delicate fluid/salt balance, which include sodium, potassium and chlorine; and those responsible for the well-being of tissues, such as calcium, phosphorus, magnesium, zinc and iron.

Nutrient intake

Table 15: *Recommended daily intake of nutrients for 18 – 35 year-olds in the UK, 1965*

Occupation	Energy requirement Calories	Protein g	B_1 mg	B_2 mg	Niacin mg	C mg	A μg	D μg	Calcium mg	Iron mg
Sedentary	2,700	68	1.1	1.7	18	30	750	2.5	500	10
Moderately active	3,000	75	1.2	1.7	18	30	750	2.5	500	10
Very active	3,600	90	1.4	1.7	18	30	750	2.5	500	10

An interesting point arising from this Table is that in terms of top-level sport 3,600 calories is not very high and some sportsmen double this figure in their training. The levels of all the vitamins, particularly vitamin C, are well down on those recommended by Russian and Finnish surveys.

Table 16: *Percentage nutrient contributions made by important foods in the average British diet*

Food Group	Calories	Protein	Fat	Calcium	Iron
Milk, cheese, eggs	15	29	21	63	6
Meat/fish	16	31	30	4	29
Cereals (bread, etc.)	31	29	11	22	8
Fruit/vegetables	10	10	1	8	22
Fats (butter, etc.)	15	1	36	1	—
Sugars/preserves	12	—	—	—	—

From Tables 13, 14 and 16 we can see the important contributions that certain food groups make to our diet. Dairy products and eggs make a massive contribution, providing at least 10% of our total Calorie requirements, about

20% of our protein and over 50% of our calcium requirements. Meat and fish make a major contribution to our total nutritional needs. Cereals provide most of the carbohydrates required, thereby contributing about 30% of our total energy needs. Cereals also contribute to our protein and vitamin intake: this is made possible by enriching flour after it has been milled. Fruit and vegetables are extremely important because of their contribution to our vitamin requirements.

If we eat well from the six basic groups indicated in Tables 14 and 16 we are certain to supply ourselves with all of the nutritional requirements which an active body could need. The simple idea of cereal-plus-egg for breakfast, and meat-or-fish-plus-vegetables for lunch and dinner, combined with the milk and sweeteners in the associated beverages, will certainly assure that our nutritional requirements are fully met. To summarise:

O each meal should contain some foods rich in protein; i.e. meat, poultry, fish, cheese, eggs, milk and bread
O each meal should contain fruit, or fruit juice, and vegetables to assure our supply of vitamins and minerals
O each meal should contain some energy-rich foods such as fats, bread, cakes, biscuits, etc., but these should only be sufficient to satisfy the appetite, to provide our energy needs and to maintain the correct body weight

OTHER CONSIDERATIONS RELATING TO NETBALL

Pre-match meal

Always rehearse the situation and keep to the foods which have proven palatable in the past. Avoid eating later than two hours prior to a match, as otherwise discomfort and a reduction in efficiency are likely. Avoid eating proteins immediately before a match as they require a long transit time through the gut. Quickly assimilated carbohydrates are the best. Many players find honey on toast, with fruit juice or sweet tea as a drink, most suitable.

A small ingestion of glucose/fructose immediately prior to a match and during the interval could prove beneficial. However, there must be caution here as a large ingestion – such as might be contained in one of the glucose drinks – could trigger off the insulin reaction, which has the effect of reducing rather than boosting energy reserves.

Netball in hot climates

In addition to the European countries involved in playing the sport, the international or touring-club player could find herself on the court in Hawaii, the West Indies, Australia or New Zealand, playing in quite unfamiliar temperatures. Playing in a very hot, humid situation will have an adverse effect upon performance. In terms of diet, the player will need to restore the electrolyte balance.

Frequently this is done by increasing the intake of carbonated drinks, a practice that should be avoided. To replace fluids lost due to the body adapting to heat one should use sterilised water, or fruit juice diluted with this water. This is merely a precaution against stomach upsets.

In terms of restoring the electrolyte balance, you should use one of the specially prepared drinks, or prescribed salt or slow-sodium tablets. Acclimatisation to this imbalance is rapid – it is fairly complete within just a few days – after which supplementation, other than to quench thirst, should not be necessary.

Travelling abroad

Lengthy journeys in aircraft can certainly have an adverse effect upon performance immediately following the trip. Precautions should be taken against overeating just to relieve boredom. During flight it is difficult to take exercise, and hence less food than usual should be consumed. However, the frequent provision of meals during such flights calls for a lot of self-discipline to decline what is often an attractive-looking meal. But do not decline the fluids likely to accompany the meal.

One should avoid eating unfamiliar foods likely to upset the stomach. Consultation with the team doctor on the use of prophylactics such as 'streptotriads' should be part of every preparation for an overseas tour. The idea of a personal medical bag, containing medicines that could help to relieve stomach upsets, etc., is a sound one, and should be explored with the help of the team's medical officer or one's own general practitioner.

CONCLUSION

Finally, we should conclude by emphasising the futility of finely tuning the human engine, adopting sophisticated training schedules and performance techniques, only to try to fuel it with low-grade food.

Chapter 10

The application of biomechanics to netball skills

Dr Adrian Lees

Dr Adrian Lees is a senior lecturer in sports science in the Department of Sport and Recreation Studies, Liverpool Polytechnic. His academic interest is in sports biomechanics, particularly the application of the computer to sport, in which area he has published widely.

INTRODUCTION

Sports biomechanics is that area of study which is concerned with an application of the mechanical laws of nature to sports skills, and with the objective measurement of these skills in physical terms.

Sports biomechanics can make two important contributions to the analysis of *individual* netball skills. Firstly, the human body can be considered as a multi-segment object and, as such, like all other physical objects, as obeying the mechanical laws of nature.

Secondly, sports biomechanics offers the methodology for making *objective* measurements of sports skills. The two main techniques with which sports biomechanics is concerned for the provision of information are cine or video film analysis and force measurement. From Newton's Laws of Motion we know that objects will move (more correctly, change their state of motion) only under the action of forces, and so if we can measure these forces we can predict the resulting movement that will occur. Cine or video film can give us a record of the movement that has occurred and allow us to make measurements of velocity, acceleration, position and angles. It can also permit us to time events or components of events and look at their sequence of occurrence.

These two techniques allow a check to be made on the application of the laws of nature which enables us to make judgements concerning the effective performance of skills.

The theory of sports biomechanics is well covered in several texts (see Bibliography, page 217), and there is no intention to repeat this here. However, it is worth noting that the core of sports biomechanics is based on Newton's three Laws of Motion. For the sake of convenience these are noted here.

O First Law: an object will remain in a state of rest or uniform motion unless some net external force acts upon it
O Second Law: an object will undergo an acceleration which is proportional to, and in the same direction as, the *net* external force acting on it
O Third Law: forces always act in pairs – the reaction force is equal and opposite to the action force

These laws can be applied in both their linear *and* angular forms, and can be extended by mathematical manipulation to cover the concepts of conservation of momentum and angular momentum, and the conservation of mechanical energy.

The insight that sports biomechanics can give to the netball coach can best be developed within a netball context. Selected netball skills can be taken in isolation and their execution viewed in biomechanical terms.

SHOOTING

Successful shooting is perhaps the most important aspect of the game of netball, since without it the game cannot be won. Success in shooting comes from the careful execution of a precision skill.

Shooting action

The typical shot is one in which the feet are comfortably placed apart, the knees are flexed, and the arms are flexed with the ball held in the dominant hand above the head. The throw is initiated by the extension of the legs with the trunk held firmly, and is concluded by a quick extension of the arm and a flick of the wrist. What is the importance of each of these actions, and how do they contribute to the final ball velocity? Measurements made on an international player of the vertical velocities of the hip (produced as a result of leg extension), the wrist (produced as a result of arm extension) and of the ball (produced as a result of wrist flick) are given in Figure 143a, for a long shot taken on the edge of the circle, and in Figure 143b, for a short shot taken under the posts.

Fig. 143a   *Fig. 143b*

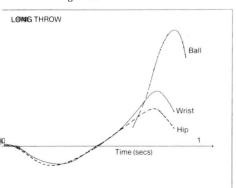

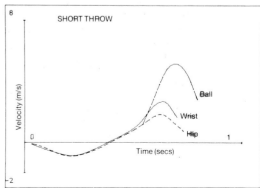

From these results several interesting points can be made concerning the execution of the skill.

○ The similarity between the curves of hip and wrist velocity over the leg flexion or preparation phase indicates that only the legs are actively involved in this.

○ In the propulsion phase, the legs first of all begin to extend, moving the bulk of the body, and then arm extension begins. The difference between the two curves over this phase is an indication of the contribution that arm extension makes to ball velocity (about 25%) for the long throw.

○ Both wrist and hip velocities peak at the same time, indicating that one velocity is building on another, which is an indication of effective performance.

○ The contribution made by wrist flexion in order to increase the ball velocity is in both throws quite marked, and indicates the importance of this action. Maximum ball velocity occurs at a slightly later time than maximum hip and wrist velocity, and contributes over 35% to the velocity of the throw.

○ For producing maximum velocity, the delay in wrist flexion would be considered as poor performance. However, the nature of this skill should be remembered: it is one of precision. The majority of velocity is built up by the legs and arm, but it is the fingers of the hand which give the final fine control to the ball direction before release as well as adding additional velocity. It is advantageous to delay wrist flexion to allow the possibility of modification of ball-release velocity.

Coaches should be aware of the importance of each component to the shooting action, and they should endeavour to develop practices which serve to draw players' attention to them. Of particular importance are the variations in shooting pattern which occur as a result of length of shot, and the role of wrist flexion in both propelling and controlling ball-release direction.

Ball trajectory

Why do coaches often ask for the ball to be projected higher into the air? One good reason for this is to make sure the ball clears the defence. Another good reason is to increase the effective target area into which the ball is directed. This can be illustrated by considering the *area* which is swept out by the ball as it travels in two different trajectories (see Figure 144). In the case of a low trajectory (*a*) there is no margin for error for a clear entry into the net, while for a high trajectory (*b*) there is a much greater margin of error (maximum 8cm [3in] each side).

How can the height of the trajectory be increased? The direction in which a ball will go at release will depend on its horizontal and vertical velocities. If we wish to increase the height of the trajectory then we must increase the vertical velocity component. This will in effect increase the angle of projection (Figure 145).

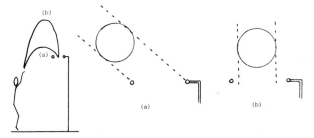

Fig. 144 By increasing the height of the shot the angle at which the ball enters the ring can be increased. This gives a greater margin for error for clear entry of the netball into the net.

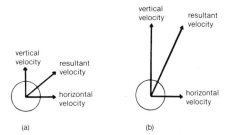

Fig. 145 Velocity components of release and their relationship with release angle. An increase in vertical velocity in (b) increases the release angle and the resultant velocity.

The vertical component of velocity can be increased by a more vigorous leg, arm and wrist action in the *vertical* direction. From the results of Figures 143a and 143b, we see that wrist flexion is likely to be the most easily utilised action for this, although both leg and arm actions should also be used to preserve the precision of the skill.

Ball spin

The wrist flick used in the shooting action naturally tends to produce backspin on the ball. When shooting a goal, the *rear* rim of the net is the target area so that, when it hits the rim, the ball will have a tendency, if it has backspin, to roll back into the net.

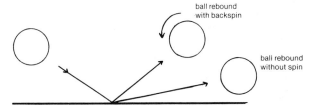

Fig. 146 The rebound can be affected by spin. Backspin can cause the ball to increase its angle of rebound from a solid surface.

There are no published figures on the speed of netball rotation, but some measurements taken by the author from high-speed cine film indicate that 1 – 2revs/sec is a reasonable figure. This would increase the rebound angle in Figure 146 by only about 7°. However, bouncing off a rim is a very different situation from bouncing off a solid surface. The nature of the rebound will depend on the point of contact of the rim on the ball *and* the direction in which the ball is travelling.

Consider first a ball/rim impact with *no* spin (Figure 147). The direction in which the ball will go (into or out of the net) is very sensitive to the initial direction of the ball and the point of contact of the ball and the rim. Clearly, in the two examples shown of low and high trajectory, the higher trajectory gives better success (this is a further reason for adopting a high trajectory). In each of the cases illustrated, backspin will have a tendency to change the rebound direction more towards the net. However, with the degree of spin available (and other factors such as the amount of skid produced on contact) it is unlikely that spin will modify the rebound path by more than about 5 – 10°. Certainly the effect of spin will be small compared with the more major effect that the point of contact of rim and ball has on the resulting direction of rebound.

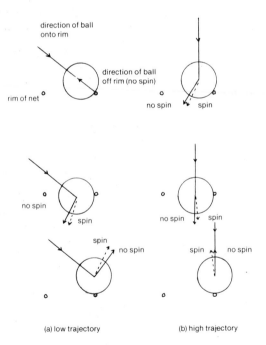

Fig. 147 Netball landing on the rim of the net for (a) low trajectory and (b) high trajectory. Comparison of rebound angles for different position of contact. The effect of the spin is indicated by the dashed arrows.

PASSING AND RECEIVING

Throwing

Different throwing techniques can be modified to take account of the distance the ball needs to be thrown. However, they are all based on one important principle, which is that the throw is initiated by the large muscle groups in the legs and sequentially followed by muscle groups in the trunk, shoulders, and finally arm and wrist. In a throw for distance the use of *all* of these muscle groups is important, as is their correct sequential timing. For shorter, more precise, throwing the legs and trunk muscles may not be used: the muscle power available in the shoulders and arms is often sufficient, and this is where the final muscular adjustments are made for accuracy.

The velocity of the throw can be increased significantly by stepping or moving into the throw. The leading foot must be firmly placed ahead of the body and the body will pivot about this point. The precise moment of release is determined and modified by the arms and hands for the required point and angle of release.

Generally speaking, a greater release velocity can be achieved by using a one-handed throw. The action is very much like a javelin throw. The point to look for in judging whether this type of throw is technically correct or not is the evidence of a 'leading elbow'. Just before release, the one-handed throw gives a greater radius of rotation of the hand and ball about the shoulder than the two-handed throw. Consequently, this will give a greater velocity for a given rotational speed produced by the legs and trunk. The type of throwing action best described as a pushing action with little trunk rotation should be avoided when throws for distance are required.

Flight path

It is well known that the resulting flight path of a projectile is determined by the height, angle and velocity of release. In addition to this, air resistance and ball spin also have their effects.

Ball spin is unlikely to have any significant effect on the flight path of the netball (as it does for example on the golf ball), because of the low spin imparted to it. C. H. Daish gives the effect of spin on the forces experienced by a sphere, and calculations based on this data show that a ball spin of 10revs/sec would have to be imparted to a netball in order to produce a noticeable movement – say 20cm over a 10m throw (6in over a 25ft throw) in the horizontal plane.

Of the three release parameters of height, angle and velocity which determine the range, the latter is the most important. The range can also be maximised for a given effort by controlling the angle of projection. In air the optimum angle of projection of a netball is not 45°, as is often thought; 40 – 42° is a more realistic value.

Receiving

To catch a ball successfully, the momentum that was imparted to the ball during the throw must be reduced. Hard, unyielding surfaces, such as a rigidly held arm and hand, should not be used for catching.

The technique of catching which allows the force to be reduced is one in which the hand stretches out for the ball and slows the ball down gradually, all the time giving with the ball in the direction that the ball is travelling. This 'giving' movement can easily be produced by a flexion of the elbow and shoulder joints.

Coaching advice often suggests a two-handed catch, and this is sound on the basis of safe receiving. However, as the competitiveness of the game develops, or if there is a serious height disadvantage, then a one-handed catch allows extra height to be gained.

Jumping

Little attention is given to the technique of jumping to gain extra height. If jumping from a static position, it is best to jump from two feet. The technique used is that of a vertical jump, where the arms are brought down to the side as the body crouches. The arms are then swung vigorously upwards, and sequentially the trunk and legs are extended. The arms are important for gaining extra height but, if they are kept above the head during the jump to secure the ball, extra attention should be given to the role of the trunk and hip extensor muscles.

If a jump is to be made on the move, then it is best performed from one leg. The leg to use is the one opposed to the preferred catching hand; e.g., the left leg if right-handed. This is because, in the natural running action, as the left leg is placed on the ground the right arm is naturally behind the body. As the jump is made the right arm can be brought through and swung into the air to aid the jumping movement.

Curiously, a running jump from one leg is superior to a static jump from two. The reason for this is thought to be due to the elastic nature of the muscles and tendons of the leg. These serve to store energy which can be released to aid the jump. The kinetic energy of the body while running is considerable, and a lot of this can be stored within the leg structure.

Receiving and throwing (catch-release)

An advanced technique in netball is to receive (catch) the ball, turn the body, and throw (release) it while still in the air (see Chapter 3).

Turning while in the air is a complicated matter. The twisting motion of the body is governed by the law of conservation of angular momentum – an extension of Newton's Second Law. What this basically says is that, if the body is in the air, then whatever angular momentum it had when it left the ground it retains until it touches the ground again. Consequently, if we wish to produce a large rotation of the body while in the air (say 180°), then the body must be turning *before* it leaves the ground.

It is possible for a small degree of rotation of the body to be produced without any twist before leaving the ground. This is done by a 'cat-twist' action – often seen performed by trampolinists. About a quarter turn can be produced this way. High-speed film of an expert player executing a half twist in the air shows that the twist is initiated on the ground (see Figure 148).

Fig. 148

ATTACKING AND DEFENDING

Successful attacking and defending rely on quick movement around the court. Territorial restrictions limit the distance over which movements can be made, and so short sharp bursts of speed with rapid changes in direction and sudden stops are the common features which can be analysed.

Speed off the mark

Analysis of 100m sprint runners shows that they do not obtain their maximum velocity until they have run about 20 – 25m (22 – 27yd) from the starting line. As distances run in netball are almost always shorter than this, the netball player is unlikely to reach maximum running speed. Of importance, however, is how quickly a player can accelerate and cover a shorter distance – say 5 or 10m (16 – 33ft) – in the shortest time.

The standing start differs in one important respect between sprinting and netball. The direction of travel in netball is not always known. Consequently in netball the feet should not only be placed apart in the forward-backward direction, but also in the lateral or side direction as well. The ankle and knees should be flexed ready for action, but the trunk kept fairly upright so that it can move in any specified direction. In cases where movement is to the side, the outward rotation which occurs as the foot extends is a strong muscular movement.

Sprinters achieve a stride frequency of nearly 4.5 strides per second. In order to achieve this, the recovery of each leg after it has driven the body forward must be rapid. It is thought that the speed of leg recovery is the major limiting factor to running speed. The leg can be brought forward more quickly by reducing its moment of inertia about the hip – that is, by flexing the knee joint maximally so that the foot is as close as possible to the hip (Figure 149). This results in the characteristic high knee lift associated with sprinters.

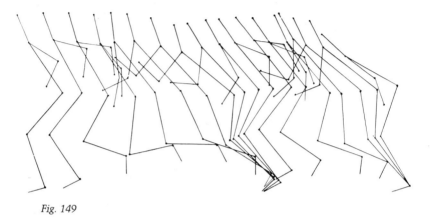

Fig. 149

Another characteristic action observed in sprinters which is firmly rooted in the laws of mechanics is the high arm action. The running action is contra-lateral (i.e., the right arm and left leg come forward at the same time), and so a vigorous leg action must be matched by a vigorous arm action in order to conserve the angular momentum and hence the balance of the body about the vertical axis.

Coaches should recognise the conflict between (*a*) using the arms to aid the running action and (*b*) their role in catching the ball. Utilizing the arms to aid running initially is important, as it would be when running *off* the ball. When speed has been obtained when running *on* the ball, the arms would more appropriately be diverted to their ball-catching role.

Stopping

Stopping is to a large degree similar to starting, in that it can only be achieved by the appropriate application of horizontal force. This horizontal force is known as the frictional or braking force, and occurs naturally on every stride in both walking and running. As the foot is placed down on the ground there is a vertical force, and this causes a frictional force opposite to the direction of motion. This force occurs because the foot is placed *in front* of the body. Therefore, if we wish to apply a larger frictional force (e.g., to stop the body more quickly), the foot must be placed *further* in front of the body (see Chapter 2).

The effect of the vertical component of force, like the frictional force, can be measured by a force platform.

Players usually find that their landing action is determined by the type of ball that they are receiving. Often this will mean that they have to jump high into the air to catch the ball and then stop. In many ways this is mechanically advantageous. Jumping into the air when on the move requires a conversion of some of the 'horizontal' kinetic energy to 'vertical' kinetic energy. This results in lower braking force being required on landing. However, due to the extra height gained the resulting vertical impact force will almost certainly be larger and so must be controlled.

When coaches are teaching the landing variations, it is important that they are aware of the mechanical principles involved and the steps they may take to reduce the effects of shock forces on the body should this be necessary.

Changing direction

Changing direction requires the application of a force in the intended direction; as in starting from rest, the greater the horizontal component of force the more quickly will the direction change take place. Therefore the leg which is being used to cause the change must be flexed ready to extend, and ought to be placed to the side of the centre of gravity. A strong driving thrust should be made in the intended direction with the leg, and also a strong outward rotation of the driving foot to push off the ball of the foot.

The feint dodge requires a reversal of the above principles. When feinting in a given direction it is important *not* to apply a large force in that direction because this will only have to be reversed again soon afterwards. It is best to create the illusion of moving by moving the parts of the body on which the defender is likely to be concentrating. These are usually the arms, shoulder and head. These can be moved relatively easily in one direction while the rest of the body is moving in the other, or by a small total body movement in one direction which will enable the driving leg to be flexed ready for an explosive drive in the opposite direction.

CONCLUSION

The principles and techniques of biomechanics can be applied to the skills of netball to give an insight into their performance. While, based on such analyses, generalisations can be made which form a sound basis for the generation of coaching points, it should be remembered that all individuals vary in their method of performance. It is the art of the coach to tailor such generalisations to specific individuals.

Chapter 11
Audiovisual resources for coaching
Andrew Wood

Andrew Wood, B.A., *is a senior lecturer at Anglia Polytechnic. He has taught in schools and colleges and has also spent some time in educational administration. He has been working in the learning resources field since 1974, and has a particular interest in the use of video as a medium for observation and training.*

The netball coach is in the communications business. She has to motivate her team to play netball to an increasingly higher standard using information and persuasion techniques which are common to communicators in all walks of life. This chapter aims to show how audiovisual resources can fit into a coaching programme and help to make communication and learning more varied, enjoyable and effective.

THE NATURE OF COMMUNICATION
Most people working in this field adopt a simple model of communication called the information-processing model. It is limited, as is any model, by the complexity of human behaviour, but it helps in understanding some of the processes involved.

Put quite simply, the coach is the source of the communication and aims to pass on a 'message' (of varying complexity) to the players. If the message is to be received and acted upon it must be in a form which the recipient will understand and it should not be altered by extraneous factors. Extraneous factors affecting a message are often called 'noise' (rather like getting a bad telephone line) and the process of checking that a message has been received is referred to as seeking 'feedback'. This model can be represented as in Figure 150.

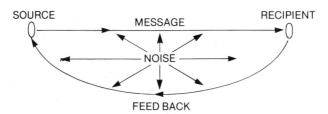

Fig. 150

The coach must ensure that conditions are suitable before attempting to convey a message, and this often means that the attention of the recipient has to be captured first then directed to the content of any communication. Audiovisual resources can often help in this process.

In the coach/player relationship the communication model is often reversed. The player also communicates with the coach, and the quality of the feedback which the coach provides is vital to the improvement of the player's performance.

Using all the senses

We receive our information about the world through a variety of channels. Many coaching programmes work on the basis that the only sense a human being possesses is that of hearing, but there are six senses: vision, hearing, touch, taste, smell and proprioception. Successful communication will take account of most of these whenever possible. In respect of netball coaching, taste and smell are less likely to be relevant.

Proprioception is the sense which tells one where one's body is placed in relation to the environment, both when stationary and during movement. A coach is using this sense whenever she demonstrates a movement skill and then asks the players to copy it. Touch is important particularly in terms of handling the ball and as it is related to proprioception.

The player clearly gains much information about the game from her eyes. The coach can build on this by using a variety of visual aids which will be dealt with shortly.

Sound has particular characteristics which mark it out from the other senses. Vision can be obliterated merely by closing the eyes, but sound cannot be switched off in this way. Information comes to the ears from all around and from different distances, so that understanding what is heard requires concentration; in other words, there is a difference between hearing and listening. The coach must 'cue' the players into listening to what she is saying.

'Open-loop' and 'closed-loop' communication

Before considering the resources available to the coach, it is important to recognise that some forms of communication work in different ways from others. 'Open-loop' communication does not allow the learner to respond in such a way that the message can be changed or reinterpreted. An example of this would be a film or television programme: it is beamed at an audience and they can take it or leave it. 'Closed-loop' communication, however, allows for feedback which can change the message as in a computer program. The coach herself is a closed-loop communicator when she is open to feedback.

Finally, by the way a coach uses it, an open-loop communication such as a film, wallchart or set of slides can be converted into a closed-loop communication when the coach herself encourages and receives feedback from the audience.

THE AUDIOVISUAL RESOURCES AVAILABLE TO THE COACH

Pictures

Still pictures can be a very effective aid, and they are usually simple for a coach to acquire and display. They can be in the form of photographs, diagrams, cuttings from magazines, or wallcharts. For best effect, photographs and cuttings should be mounted on light card using a suitable glue or spray mount. Pictures can be grouped into a series as a wallchart to show the development of particular skills.

In selecting pictures and designing wallcharts bear in mind that too much information can interfere with the particular message that needs to be put across. Keep the amount of detail down to that which is required to convey the message.

Pictures and wallcharts can be displayed in sports halls, changing rooms and even on general noticeboards, where they will be seen frequently and regularly. This will ensure that the message is reinforced over a period of time. Equally, when conducting an indoor session a coach can use pictures to reinforce and elaborate what she is saying. There is no reason why they should not also be used on the court, but it would be sensible to have a case in which to keep them and to protect them with a clear waterproof covering such as acetate.

Handouts

Handouts can be useful, particularly for information which needs to be referred to frequently. The three main ways of producing these are by using (a) a spirit duplicator, (b) an ink duplicator, (c) a photocopier. In producing handouts, remember not to concentrate the information too heavily but to spread it out over the page, divide it into sections and use clear diagrams where relevant.

Audio-cassette recorders

The use of sound for netball coaching is not immediately obvious, but you may like to consider three possibilities. The first is as a musical accompaniment to certain warming-up exercises. Music imparts a rhythm and relaxation to such exercises which can benefit their effect considerably.

The second way of using a portable recorder is as a feedback device to enable you to criticise your own coaching techniques. All you need to do is leave the recorder in the recording mode at a strategic place by the court and listen to the results in privacy later. It may take one or two tries in order to place the microphone correctly, but your voice is likely to be the dominant sound when you use it and it should depress the other background sounds. When making an analysis of your performance try to bear in mind the points made about communication earlier in this chapter.

A third possibility is to use one of the small micro-cassette recorders as a substitute for taking notes. This can be particularly useful when watching match play, as one can record one's impressions verbally without taking one's eyes off the court.

Projected resources

Projected resources can be a most effective means of communication when they are correctly used. The three main types of projector which are generally available are the overhead projector, the filmstrip/slide projector and the film projector.

Overhead projector

The overhead projector (OHP) is a simple piece of apparatus but provides a variety of creative opportunities to present information of the kind that could be useful to coaches, such as illustrating positioning on the court and simple team tactics.

It was primarily designed to replace the blackboard, and its special advantages include the following:

O   it projects a bright image onto a high screen
O   it contains a roll of acetate which can be moved forwards or backwards in order to recapitulate on a session
O   one can write on the acetate roll in a variety of bright colours
O   one can prepare individual transparencies which can be used again and again (like the outline of a netball court)
O   one can face the group while one is talking

The filmstrip/slide projector

This piece of apparatus is quite commonly available, and many of us have one in our homes. Most people planning to use a projector find it very helpful to get their slides in the right order and position for projection in advance of actually using the projector. With a filmstrip it is advisable to load it onto the projector in advance and check that it is going to be projected correctly.

The film projector

There are two main types of film projector in common use: the 16mm and the 8mm.

The operation of cine projectors is such a source of anxiety to most people that it prevents them from ever considering the use of a film. Consequently the enormous power of colour, movement and sound which is the hallmark of this medium is seldom employed to bring about effective learning. Because cine projection is very much a practical skill and each projector is slightly different, it is not possible to teach the art in a handbook like this. Nevertheless, the reader is urged to find someone in a local school, college or business who will spend a little time showing them how to use a projector.

Video-cassette recorders

Video is one of the fastest growing media of communication and its potential as an aid to coaching is considerable.

As a replay device, the video-cassette recorder (VCR) is limited only by the software (i.e., video-cassettes) which is available. The AENA will be considering the production of a coaching video-cassette in the near future but, at present, the main sources of relevant material are recordings of international matches broadcast on television and the occasional programme about the game in general TV series on sport.

The VCR is a particularly flexible device for teaching the skills of the game because of the features that are now standard on most models. These enable you to freeze the action, to speed it up (backwards or forwards) and to slow it down. This enables the coach to analyse skills and tactics in considerable depth with a group of players, and crucial elements can be viewed as often as is necessary to ensure that they have been understood. The purpose is to use the medium not to entertain but to communicate quite specific coaching points more effectively than can be done by other means.

So far we have looked at video as a medium for playback, but it is possible to use a video camera and portable recorder or one-piece camcorder to preserve material for your own use. The major manufacturers are currently developing systems which will be sold even more cheaply in the near future.

Remember that a good picture requires three things: sufficient light, a steady support for the camera and correct picture composition.

For most purposes the camera should be mounted on a good tripod with a smooth action. Most video cameras have a powerful zoom lens which enables one to get good action close-ups, but when the lens is zoomed in camera shake is also magnified. A good tripod will eliminate this.

Picture composition is important, not for artistic reasons but because the camera must be pointed at those parts of the action which the coach wants to analyse later with the players. A couple of examples may help to guide your first attempts. After that results will improve with experience.

Recording the skill of shooting

First the camera needs to be positioned so that it captures the action from the direction you want it to be viewed. Next the lens needs to be set so that it will remain focused during the whole process to be viewed.

Then a decision has to be taken as to how much of the player is to be in shot. Do you want to concentrate on the head, arms and shoulders, or do you want to see the player's body from head to toe? If the latter is the case, have you got enough light to ensure sharp detail on the picture? After setting the zoom lens to accommodate the amount of the player's body you wish to record you are ready to shoot.

At this point the advantage of using video rather than cine film becomes apparent, because one can shoot the scene again and again until one is satisfied without worrying about the cost of film.

Recording a team moving up the court while retaining control of the ball through passing

Again the camera needs to be positioned so that it can capture all the action. In this case you may wish to place the camera high up, so that the players nearest the lens do not obscure what is going on in other parts of the court.

Bear in mind that, although an experienced coach can follow the speed of such a manoeuvre and separate out important details from the inessential, this is not so easy for an inexperienced player. So, particularly if you are recording a demonstration, it may be a good idea to reduce the number of players on the court to perhaps three attackers and two defenders. This will ensure that there is not too much detail in the picture and avoid confusing the less experienced player.

As before, the lens needs to be focused on the area of action and the zoom set to capture the amount of detail you want (say two players at any one time).

MICROCOMPUTERS

The arrival of cheap but powerful microcomputers has provided an additional aid to the coach, but the application of this technology to sports coaching generally is still in its infancy. The screen lay-out of the best microcomputers makes them relatively easy to use, even by those with no previous experience. By using a 'mouse' to control the information on the screen there is no need to have keyboard skills before you can use a computer program.

The netball coach could use a microcomputer in two ways. Firstly, as another aid to communication: some of the skills and tactics of the game could be distilled into computer simulation programs for use with a group of players or by individuals. Secondly, it could be used for processing the variety of information that a coach deals with, such as analysis of player characteristics and performance.

In addition, it could be used for storing administrative information such as names and addresses or times and dates of matches. Finally, if the video-games manufacturers design a netball cartridge this could be a valuable training aid, particularly with regard to team tactics.

ESTABLISHING A RESOURCES CENTRE

Experience in schools, colleges and business-training departments has shown that the most effective way of encouraging the use of the audiovisual resources described in this chapter is to set up a resources centre. It enables equipment such as projectors and screens to be permanently set up, and provides a focus for a range of activities and initiatives. Books and magazines can be made easily available; pictures, notices and wallcharts can be displayed; and it is even possible to arrange for individuals to view slides, films and video-cassettes.

CONCLUSION

The main purpose of this chapter has been to encourage netball coaches, whatever their experience of using audiovisual resources, to experiment with them and to evaluate the usefulness of them to their own coaching programmes.

Chapter 12
Measurement and evaluation in netball

Brian Miller

Brian Miller, B. ED. (HONS.), *is on the staff at the Australian Institute of Sport, Canberra, Australia. He is a physical-education specialist who has had over twenty papers published in Australia, the USA and Canada. His principal research interests centre on his work as a sports psychology consultant for Sports Psychology Associates. In this capacity he is responsible for the mental preparation of many Olympic and international sportsmen and women in Britain, including the England Netball squad.*

An overriding principle governing the actions of a netball coach must be the all-round improvement of players in her team or squad. In order to achieve this, a coach should be willing and able to monitor, evaluate and assess the progress of her players.

According to Battles and Odom in their paper 'Predictor Variables', 'Selecting the athletes who will contribute to team success is perhaps the most important and difficult decision a coach will make.' Obviously, a team which has only seven available players is unlikely to be faced with such problems, but this is just one example of the type of decision a coach will have to make during the course of a season.

While the following observation (from this author's 'Tests and Measurement in the Assessment of Athletic Ability') was originally directed towards coaches of athletics, it is of equal relevance to those working in netball. 'In the coaching and preparation of athletes, a coach has to make many decisions concerning the training and performance of his or her charges. Since many of these decisions affect athletes there is an obvious need for objectivity and rationality. As more information is gathered relevant to an issue, the objectivity of decision-making is enhanced. The processes of measurement and evaluation allow coaches to reduce their reliance on subjective opinion in assessing athletic training.'

The process of *assessment* involves both measurement and evaluation. *Measurement* is the process of assigning numbers to properties of an individual – for example, vertical jumping ability measured in centimetres. *Evaluation* is the process of making judgements about the results of such measurement. These processes can be closely related to the nature of netball and as such it seemed reasonable to develop a model which reflected the contributing factors to success in netball (Figure 151).

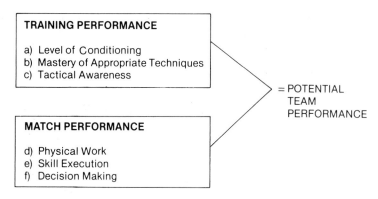

Fig. 151 Assessment in netball

The three factors under the heading 'training performance' in Figure 151 are each mirrored by those contained in match performance. The level of conditioning that a player possesses is likely to influence strongly the amount of physical work (running, jumping, etc.) she will do in a match. The degree of technique mastery will influence the final skill execution when placed under the pressure of match conditions. Basic tactical awareness is obviously a major contributing factor to the decision-making that subsequently occurs in a given match.

It is proposed that assessment in netball should logically be divided into two sections which reflect the division adopted within the model.

ANALYSIS OF TRAINING PERFORMANCE

Level of conditioning

Chapter 7 of this book deals with the physiological demands of netball, and four of the so called five 's' factors are relevant in this context. Speed, strength, stamina and suppleness are all components of physical conditioning, and a coach can take a crude measure of these in the training environment.

Strength is typically measured by performance in standardised weight-training exercises or by explosive gross body movements such as the standing broad-jump.

Speed, by comparison, is measured over a relatively short distance (40 – 60m [44 – 66yd]), or combined with agility and assessed over a series of shuttle-runs (4 × 10m [4 × 11yd]).

Stamina is a double-edged sword comprising cardiorespiratory and endurance factors. Cardiorespiratory qualities are usually measured by the distance covered in a 12-minute run, and endurance can be measured by the number of repetitions (of sit-ups, press-ups, burpees) performed in a 30- or 60-second period.

Suppleness may be measured with the use of a flexometer or other physiological apparatus. However, the club coach is more likely to rely upon her own observational skills during warm-up sessions. Players who are unable to reach adequate mobility positions (see photographs below) may require a programme of 'remedial' exercises.

Mastery of appropriate techniques

Australian-based lecturers Helen Parker (in 1977 and 1981) and Pamela Barham and Noela Wilson (in 1981) have produced very interesting papers concerning skill assessment in netball. The 'average' coach or physical-education teacher may not be in a position to use their proposed skill tests due to constraints of space, equipment or time. Nevertheless, the articles are well worth reading and it may be that coaches could adapt the tests to fit their own circumstances. County, regional and national coaches could undoubtedly benefit from employing the originals.

Provided the tests are conducted in a consistent and standardised manner, and that the test measures an appropriate technique – e.g., one-handed passes for accuracy – then the coach can easily devise her own battery of tests. One such test, based upon Barham and Wilson's paper, and modified in Bedford, contains elements of passing, agility and footwork. The design of the test is shown in Figure 152 and photographs facing.

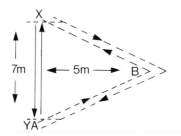

Fig. 152 The Bedford 'pass-and-go' test

Players work in threes, and at any one time two act as passive receivers while one acts as the working subject. On the command 'go' the subject passes the ball from position A to player X and runs as fast as possible around the goalpost at B (it might be a tracksuit top or rounders post where large numbers are involved) to take the ball from X's hands. The subject then passes the ball to Y and returns via the goalpost to position A. A completed circuit counts as 'one'. Depending upon the time of the season and the age and standard of the players, a coach should record the number of successful circuits completed in either 30 or 60 seconds.

The passive catchers must remain behind their restraining lines throughout the activity. They may move their bodies and arms to assist the subject, but their feet must stay behind the line. If a receiver cannot legally catch the ball because of an inaccurate pass the trial stops. The players rotate positions and each player takes her turn as the subject.

As with the test of physical conditioning, this type of activity is best employed in a longitudinal manner, whereby a player may compare her performance with previous attempts. Apart from generating useful data for the coach, such tests act as motivational aids if used spasmodically during the course of the season. Additionally, by themselves they can be purposeful skill practices.

As a cautionary note, coaches are guided towards the results of H. Parker (see Bibliography, page 219) when she examined skill tests with players of different abilities. When conducted in isolation the results obtained in a chest-passing task revealed only very small differences between players of known high standards and players of much lower abilities. It was only when this task was repeated and players were asked to perform a visual scanning task concurrently with the passing that the different standards became evident.

Therefore, while advocating the inclusion of objective skill tests in the training programme, one should add that coaches must not fall into the trap of basing all decisions (for example, team selection) upon such data. The assessment process is a coaching aid, not a panacea for all ills. Such data might be used to confirm that a younger player is truly ready to graduate into a senior side or that a more mature player is finally beginning to lose the 'edge', but they cannot be used as a complete substitute for the coach in decision-making processes.

Tactical awareness

Objective measurement and evaluation of tactical awareness and other related factors is very difficult. While a handful of colleges and universities possess an expensive piece of apparatus known as a tachistoscope (see photographs below) which may be used effectively in experiments to determine such attributes, few netball coaches will be afforded such luxuries. The tachistoscope presents slides depicting hypothetical netball situations, and players are asked what actions they would take if put in such a position.

In all probability, coaches and teachers will be able to assess such qualities only by observing practice sessions and conditioned games. This emphasises the need for astute observation on the coach's part. She must be able to observe in a slightly clinical manner and identify those players who cannot 'read the game'. A key asset is likely to be her ability to observe and make sense of what she sees.

Where appropriate, a remedial approach may be adopted with the player who cannot apply herself to the tactical situation. This would logically suggest that coaches should encourage tactical discussions and outline principles of play. It is not enough to teach techniques without transmitting the knowledge of when to employ them. This author, in 'Visual Factors in Netball Performance', has outlined the factors which influence this process in netball:

'Netball is a fast team game in which the visual display (what a player can see) is constantly changing. The ball, team-mates and opponents are always on the move. For an individual to make much sense of what is going on in such an environment, she has to process information. She needs to recognise what she sees (a team-mate in a free space), she has to make a decision (pass or not pass) and she has to execute this response (the physical act of passing). In a match, of course, this sequence does not occur in isolation. There is a great deal of movement or uncertainty, and a player may need to cancel or modify a proposed plan of action.'

ANALYSIS OF MATCH PERFORMANCE

Physical work

There have been many attempts, in a variety of sports, to record objectively the physical work of individuals in competitive situations (see the papers by Knowles and Brooke, Reilly and Thomas, and Allison listed in the Bibliography, page 218). The most common approach is to employ a spatial grid analysis and record all of the movements on court of one particular player. Ideally, a coach would want to look at all movements of all players, but realistically this would require a whole team of additional helpers/researchers.

The normal method is to devise a shorthand system to depict where, when and how a player moves on court. For instance, a zig-zag line might represent sprinting and an arrow-head on that line would indicate the direction of movement. A number of small-scale courts would be drawn on sheets of paper, and the recorder might use one court to represent one minute's play. If only one court were used per match, then there would be an overload of information on one display. Figures 153 and 154 (page 202) would appear to be a sensible compromise.

While such an approach can yield valuable information, it relies heavily upon instantaneous interpretation by an individual. The observer has to try and see all movements and record them accurately at the same time. This involves a succession of head motions, and in all probability some detail will be missed, misinterpreted or wrongly recorded.

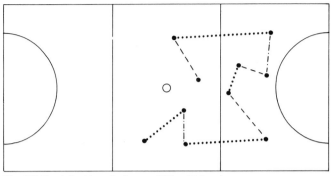

Fig. 153 Spatial grid analysis: WA, 10th – 11th minute

Key

•••••••••••• = sprinting

— — — — — = running

— · — · — · — = jogging

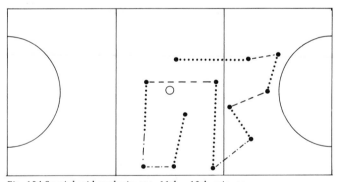

Fig. 154 Spatial grid analysis: WA, 11th – 12th minute

Fortunately, twentieth-century technology offers at least two viable alternatives. It is relatively simple to sit by the side of a court and make a verbal record of the same movement patterns by using a portable audio-cassette recorder. The cassette may subsequently be replayed at a later date and an accurate account of the physical work can be transcribed.

The second alternative, video recording, is more expensive but certainly offers a true record of what a player actually does on court. (See Chapter 11 for further details.) An advantage of this system is that it allows the player concerned to review her own output at a later session, in the presence of the coach.

Skill execution

The assessment of skill execution in match situations needs to be as objective as possible. To illustrate this point, one example of a check-off list will be examined, as well as the AENA official scoresheet.

As with the assessment of physical work, a coach would ideally like to know exactly what every player in her team has done in a game. In reality, however, time constraints suggest that for any given period of time it would be more sensible to focus attention on an individual and one category of skills. Figure 155 illustrates a possible approach.

The coding system needs to be kept simple: in Figure 155

✓ means completely successful

/ means mildly successful (e.g., the pass did reach the GS, but only because she stretched with great athleticism)

X depicts a failure

PLAYER Jo Smith		POSITION W A	OPPONENTS Lansdowne Ladies	
DATE 2/4/83 SKILL CATEGORY Handling		WEATHER CONDITIONS Fine		

	PASSES	CATCHES	INTERCEPTIONS
FIRST QUARTER	✓ ✓ / ✓ ✓ X X / ✓ ✓ ✓ X ✓ X	✓ ✓ ✓ ✓ ✓ ✓ ✓ ✓ ✓ ✓ ✓ ✓ ✓ ✓ ✓	X X / ✓

Fig. 155 Analysing skill execution

Obviously, experienced coaches could devise variations on this theme and, provided they are concise and consistent, then they should be of benefit to coaches and players alike. The techniques proposed by Embrey and Barham (see Bibliography, page 218) would offer a great deal of information to coaches, but in the first instance they are likely to be a little too intricate to use. Experienced coaches with willing and able observers might care to examine these two articles and try to implement the systems outlined. Once again, the cassette and/or video recorder might be a useful supplement to this approach.

The AENA Official Scoresheet (see Figure 156, page 204) has its limitations in terms of the information it yields, but it is particularly useful when considering the skill execution of the GS and GA. A simple system of dots and ticks can show how many goals were scored in each quarter by each player, as well as the unsuccessful attempts. With the use of a calculator, shooting percentages may be analysed throughout the season. The major

Official Scoresheet

Used in compliance with the Code of Rules of the International Federation of Netball Associations. Copyright AENA 1976

SHEET No.

		FIRST QUARTER					SECOND QUARTER					THIRD QUARTER					FOURTH QUARTER			

Tournament:

Match: YOUNG ENGLAND

Versus BARBADOS

Date 4-12 **Time**

Venue BRICKET WOOD

TEAM A: YOUNG ENGLAND
PLAYERS AT BEGINNING OF MATCH

GS	R. EDBROOKE	
GA	S. WILLIAMS	
WA	D. BAIRD	
C	G. BOOTH	
WD	D. MAHONEY	
GD	G. WHITE (c)	
GK	S. RODNEY	

CHANGES IN TEAM DURING MATCH

S. RODNEY - OFF
K. LOWE - GK

TEAM B: BARBADOS
PLAYERS AT BEGINNING OF MATCH

GS	S. BANFIELD	
GA	C. MAYERS	
WA	P. ROBERTS (c)	
C	M. HOLLINGSWORTH	
WD	M. HALL	
GD	J. BOYCE	
GK	H. WALTHE	

CHANGES IN TEAM DURING MATCH

	FIRST Q				SECOND Q				THIRD Q				FOURTH Q			
ATTEMPTS	14	3	5	3	9	7	9	12	10	1	6	4	13	4	7	5
SCORED	8	2	2	2	2	5	8	9	7	1	2	3	9	0	7	4
QUARTER SCORE	10		4		7		17		8		5		9		11	
PROGRESSIVE SCORE	10		4		17		21		25		26		34		37	

UMPIRE 1.
UMPIRE 2.
SCORER 1. C Maylor
SCORER 2
TIMEKEEPER 1
TIMEKEEPER 2

TEAM.	YOUNG ENGLAND										TEAM.	BARBADOS								
1	2	3	4	5	6	7	8	9	10		1	2	3	4	5	6	7	8	9	10
11	12	13	14	15	16	17	18	19	20		11	12	13	14	15	16	17	18	19	20
21	22	23	24	25	26	27	28	29	30		21	22	23	24	25	26	27	28	29	30
31	32	33	34	35	36	37	38	39	40		31	32	33	34	35	36	37	38	39	40
41	42	43	44	45	46	47	48	49	50		41	42	43	44	45	46	47	48	49	50
51	52	53	54	55	56	57	58	59	60		51	52	53	54	55	56	57	58	59	60
61	62	63	64	65	66	67	68	69	70		61	62	63	64	65	66	67	68	69	70
71	72	73	74	75	76	77	78	79	80		71	72	73	74	75	76	77	78	79	80
81	82	83	84	85	86	87	88	89	90		81	82	83	84	85	86	87	88	89	90
91	92	93	94	95	96	97	98	99	100		91	92	93	94	95	96	97	98	99	100

GOAL SHOOTER		GOAL ATTACK		GOAL SHOOTER		GOAL ATTACK	
ATTEMPTS:	46	ATTEMPTS:	15	ATTEMPTS:	27	ATTEMPTS:	24
SCORED:	26	SCORED:	8	SCORED:	19	SCORED:	18

MATCH WON BY: BARBADOS

FINAL SCORE 37-34

| = goal scored
• = missed attempt
0 = penalty

Designed and Printed by J W DUNN (PRINTERS) LTD CHEAM SURREY

Fig. 156

limitation in such an approach is that there is no way to record the distance from which shots were taken. A 50% average from 3m is obviously not as bad as a 50% average from 1m.

When using either of the two coding systems outlined, it must be remembered that netball is an invasive team game in which the opposition try to 'spoil the fun'. It is not a game played in isolation, and as such the standard of opposition has to be taken into account. For instance, an outstanding GK in one particular match might frustrate the attacking combination and the shooting percentage is likely to be reduced. A coach needs to supplement these objective assessment systems with her own astute observation of the prevailing conditions.

Decision-making

Decision-making in the game is closely related to the concept of tactical awareness exhibited in training sessions. In a similar way, it is very difficult to assess such an ability accurately. While attempts could be made to use crude check-off lists to identify situations where, for example, a player failed to go for an interception at the vital moment, such a system becomes quite subjective. The only satisfactory solution is to employ a video recording of the match. If the camera can be raised a little (a balcony in a sportshall, for instance), then subsequent playback will be more easily analysed and a greater appreciation of the decision-making processes will be facilitated.

CONCLUSION

To conclude this chapter, it needs to be stressed that measurement and evaluation are but the beginnings of effective coaching. The art of coaching is to assess any data gleaned from this process and apply it to the coaching session. At a practical level, this might include a 15-minute slot in the session devoted to individual or pairs practice. In this section, areas of individual weakness might be emphasised in an attempt to raise the overall standard of a squad.

Measurement and evaluation are merely tools placed at the disposal of coaches, and it is the application of such knowledge that will make the difference between the good and the merely competent coach.

Chapter 13

Netball team selection

Irene Beagles and Heather Crouch

Irene Beagles and Heather Crouch worked together with the England Netball Teams from 1980 to 1983. Both were England selectors.

There are many different procedures and systems for selecting netball teams and squads. Whether selecting at school, club, county, regional or national level, specific questions should be asked.

O Is a *squad* required? If so, what size (10, 20 or 30 players)? For what purpose? To tour, to play in a specific tournament, or to play in a league?
   To stay together for how long?
   How important is the 'balance' of the squad with regard to such factors as ability, age, experience and potential?

O Is a *team* required? If so, for what purpose? (To play a particular match? To offer experience to certain inexperienced players?)
   How long will the team stay together?
   Should the most skilful individuals be selected, or those who combine together well?
   Is a team plus reserves required, or an interchangeable squad?

All sorts of additional factors can also affect the decisions of selectors. For example, the selection of a team/squad might be

O for a games lesson or practice (when teams might need to be 'even')
O for a 'one-off' match against specific opponents
O for a season, where squad coaching will occur and teams will be regularly reselected
O when no coaching will be offered
O when teams have to be named and fixed for the season
O when additional players can be added at subsequent training sessions

As well as paying attention to the present ability of players, selectors may also need to take into account potential ability, match experience, consistency, determination, creativity, courage and temperament, as well as response to other players, to the coach and to match conditions.
Some of this information may only be available if the selection panel

includes at least one person who knows something of the background and match play of the players. For this reason, it seems sensible to include the coach as one of the selectors, especially if she will be working with the players once they have been selected.

SELECTION PROCEDURES

Selection procedures will be influenced by all these considerations as well as practical issues, such as the size of the area from which the players are being drawn (local district, county, region, country), the geographic spread of the trialists, and the existing and future netballing calendar. For example, some countries select their national teams during a week of interprovincial competition while others hold annual trials of only two days' duration. In very small countries, where most of the playing population is centred around the main towns, national selection can be relatively easy, as most of the trialists will be known to the selectors. The procedure here can be to maintain the main squad while inviting individuals, as they are 'spotted', to join the group; players who do not maintain their standard of play are simply not invited to subsequent practices. In countries of great size, the problem of bringing together players from all parts to one central point can be both expensive and time-consuming. In general, such countries decide on holding trials and team training only in preparation for major international matches and the World Tournament. These selection procedures, or adaptations of them, could well be appropriate for regional, county and even club trials.

The size of the selection committee also varies worldwide, with some countries having as many as seven members while others allow the national team coach to have the sole right to decide the national team. Selectors, however many, and at whatever level, will be looking for a number of qualities. These will include commitment to winning; perseverence in working hard for the whole match in both attack and defence; courage in making supreme physical efforts; skill in performance, showing well coordinated movement; knowledge of the role of the position being played; tactical awareness; and an awareness of one's own team and of the opposition.

INDIVIDUAL QUALITIES

There are three main criteria which can be acknowledged when selecting players for team games. These are: (a) fitness for the particular sport, which will relate to speed, strength and stamina; (b) mechanical ability, that is, the ability to perform the techniques of the skills of the game; and (c) decision-making, that is, when, where and how to perform the skills of the game, and the ability to take part in the tactical use of those skills.

In netball, as in other team games, particular positions demand specific qualities in addition to the more general qualities. These can be defined and used as a guide when comparing one player with another.

Goal Shooter

The Goal Shooter should want to shoot and be able to achieve a good goal average (approximately 80%) during match play. At times when the attempted shot is unsuccessful the ability to achieve the rebound should be apparent. The player should be constantly aware of her position in the goal circle, and should be able to take advantage of any opportunity which allows her to move towards the goal-post. She should have an awareness of her relationship with Goal Attack and should understand the important use that these two players can make of the space in the circle. Her ball handling needs to be of a high standard so that the rest of the team feel confident in feeding the ball into the circle; this, in turn, links closely with her availability to receive the pass. She should be willing to defend.

Goal Attack

The ability of Goal Attack to make the correct pass to Goal Shooter is of paramount importance, along with her awareness of the space in the circle. She should know when, where and how to release the feed ball, or receive the ball back from GS. Good peripheral vision is essential. She should be able to link tactically with either Wing Attack or Centre in achieving a fast attack on the goal when necessary and, like the Goal Shooter, she should want to score, and should have the scoring ability which demands close attention by the opposing Goal Defence. Her repartee with Goal Shooter should be constant and, while her ball handling should show variety and accuracy, the ability to jump to gain the rebound has to be within her vocabulary of skills. Again like Goal Shooter, she needs to understand the use of the space behind the back-line to achieve interplay with her partner in the circle and a position of advantage at the goal-post. She must be persistent in defence.

Wing Attack

Selectors should be looking for a Wing Attack who can receive the centre pass safely and can release the ball with speed and accuracy when required, as well as have control of both the ball and her body movement as the situation demands. Her ability to maintain and create space is of special importance, but the most crucial facet of her skill has to be in the area of her recognition of the space through which she can pass the ball to allow the shooters a shot for goal as near to the post as possible. She should be ready to back up the circle play for either a wall pass or to retrieve a loose ball from a mis-shot. She must be able to switch quickly from attacking to defending.

Centre

Since the Centre has to initiate the attack repeatedly throughout the game of netball, she needs to show accuracy and confidence in releasing the ball at the centre-pass situation. She has to show great stamina in both attack and defence, and her use of speed throughout the game should be positive, providing a confident link between the defending players and the attack. Her awareness of space is essential in that she should understand when, and when *not*, to demand the ball. She should be able to feed the circle accurately and to defend when needed. She should back up round the attacking and defending circles. Of all the players in the team, it is Centre who has to show the greatest degree of variety in almost all the skills of the game.

Wing Defence

The dogged determination required by the Wing Defence has often been described as the most demanding feature of her play. Obviously the ability to intercept the pass rates high as one of her skills, but it is usually the result of her hard work and concentration that brings this about. She has to show an aptitude for switching quickly from defence to attack, as well as the ability to change from marking the pass at the receiving end to marking that at the throwing end and, even then, changing to marking the space through which either the ball or the player may pass. In her tactical awareness she needs to understand the importance of forcing the Wing Attack to attempt to feed the ball to the goal circle from a distance, thereby creating a greater margin of error. She must achieve all this without causing contact or obstruction. She must also be able to initiate attacking play, particularly from a back-line throw-in or rebound situation.

Goal Defence

An ability to intercept the pass is again important for Goal Defence, but with the added skills of being able to upset the shooting action and intercept the shot for goal. Goal Defence should be capable of marking Goal Attack away from the goal circle, knowing that by doing so she can protect her own goal area and that her effort may well bring about a break in the Goal Attack's rhythm. She should be capable in all methods of defence, both in and out of the circle, and an ability to read the game in terms of closing down the space through which an attack may evolve is necessary. The Goal Defence should show confidence in attack, often initiating a move which will create space. Her passing should be accurate and appropriate even under stress. Her relationship with Goal Keeper should be evident, in that she is seen constantly to be communicating with her. Her awareness of the space in the circle and of her interchange with Goal Keeper in controlling that space is most important.

Goal Keeper

It should be apparent to the selector that the Goal Keeper recognises that her primary function is to protect the goal. She should be capable of marking the Goal Shooter away from the post, forcing her to attempt long shots. Of great importance is the ability to move in a confined area without making contact and to gain interceptions (without obstruction) and rebounds from the goal-post. She should be able to control the defence in general, communicating relevant information to both Goal Defence and Wing Defence. She should look confident in taking the back-line throw-in, initiating a safe attacking move using accurate passing.

In summarising the qualities for which a selector would be looking, the attacking players should demonstrate fast, accurate footwork and passing, space awareness, and flairful use of any opportunity to score a goal; while the defence should show concentrated marking, interception ability, and an acute awareness of goal protection.

TRIALS

Some of the procedures for selection have already been discussed. Probably the most common in this country is still, at whatever level, for a number of players to be called together to attend trials. This procedure involves the selectors putting individuals, usually of varying abilities, into teams to play together in team combinations which invariably have never been tried before. The purpose of this random grouping of players is to allow the selectors to identify broad categories of players which could be called 'probables', 'possibles' and 'unlikelies' – or As, Bs and Cs.

Of course, at this stage careful records should be kept of who plays *with* whom and who plays *against* whom. For example, a Wing Attack might appear particularly promising, but in fact have been always teamed in her trial games with the 'best' shooters and/or Centre. Similarly, a Goal Keeper might seem outstanding, but in each of her trial games have been playing against 'unlikely' shooters – or perhaps the Wing Attack, feeding even a good shooter, was poor.

As well as recording how many games each trialist plays, the selection panel should be aware of the *spread* of games for any one individual. For example, one player may play three or four games consecutively (especially if she was a late substitution for an absent trialist), whereas another could rest for as many as five games. This imbalance is to be deplored and can invariably be redressed if the selection panel are aware of, and know how to attend to, the problem.

Identifying the broad bands of distinction between players should be a relatively easy task. Closer scrutiny of players can now be made while trialists play in team combinations of comparable ability. Even within the group of 'probables', the 'best', 'average' and 'worst' can be distinguished, and adjustments to 'possibles' and 'unlikelies' may need to be made. The selection task now becomes increasingly difficult, and the precise problem of trying to select one of two (or more) players who appear to perform to a similar standard is rarely easy.

Some form of objective assessment may then be useful. Let us take for example the case of two wing attacks who have very similar attributes in relation to their roles in the team. Assuming that both players are aware of all the team plans, a number of comparisons can be made. But these can be made only when the team back-up is consistent and the opposition and length of playing time on court is the same for both trialists. Even then there will be some inconsistencies, for some degree of fatigue may affect either the opposition or the team in which the trialists are performing. The following observations may be charted.

O readiness for the centre pass; stance at the 'third' line; weight distribution; cues for the Centre to make decisions about the pass

O judgement of the speed and situation

O ease with which the pass is taken

O space in which the pass was achieved

O success in releasing the ball to the next attacking player; use of 'catch-release' technique, appropriateness of the pass and so on

O follow-up move

O feed to the goal circle

O response to defending; speed of changing from attack to defence

O marking ability and interception

To record all these points accurately it would be necessary to draw up a chart and perhaps to involve a number of observers in the recording process. An example of such a chart is shown in Figure 157 (page 212). This chart relates to the Wing Attack position; it is clear that specific positions demand specific references within the chart. In other words, the chart for recording the vital points about a Wing Attack would differ considerably from the chart for a Goal Defence.

Of course, further observations could be included on such a chart to give even more information. For example, the number of passes made in repartee with the shooters could be recorded, or the number of 'tips' rather than inter-ceptions. It is one of the tasks of the coach and other selectors to identify the qualities required for each playing position. Observation charts will therefore not be standardised, since various coaches and selection panels may lay emphasis on different criteria.

The information taken from the chart illustrated in Figure 156 shows that the Wing Attack achieved eight out of ten centre passes, of which six were taken in open space, possibly away from the defending Wing Defence, and four were attempted (two successfully) within limited space and possibly with difficulty. On receiving the centre pass the Wing Attack released the ball five times appropriately to the next attacking player but three times she made an inappropriate pass, either in terms of the type of pass she used or in terms of which player she used. She then followed-up her attacking pass within the correct space seven times to achieve an advantageous place at the edge of the goal circle, but three times her follow-up move could be criticised, since she was too slow on two occasions and moved through the wrong space once. The Wing Attack made seven successful passes into the goal circle out of a possible ten, of which two showed flair, four were accurate, four were given confidently and four passes were made to the shooter near to the goal-post. On three occasions she made inaccurate passes, three passes were made to the shooter away from the goal-post, and on one occasion the Wing Attack looked uncertain. Furthermore, it can be seen that she showed good repartee with the circle players and responded well when defending, making three interceptions. She had one throw-up and was successful, showed good timing and was available to play her part in court linkage. However, although she marked her player well she still needed to work on the marking of the space.

If such charts are completed on a number of occasions some differences

Readiness		Release		Follow-up	
Good	**Poor**	**Good**	**Poor**	**Good**	**Poor**
Good space ✓✓✓✓✓✓	Space limited ✓✓✓✓ 4	Apt ✓✓✓✓✓ 5	Inapt ✓✓✓ 3	Advantageous ✓✓✓✓✓✓✓ 7	Too slow ✓✓ 2 Wrong space ✓ 1

Centre pass ✓✓✓✓ x ✓✓ x ✓✓				**Total** 8/10	

Feed to Circle ✓✓✓✓ x ✓✓✓ x x			**Total** 7/10	

Flairful	✓✓	2	Uncertain	✓	1
Accurate	✓✓✓✓	4	Inaccurate	✓✓✓	3
Near goal-post	✓✓✓✓	4	Away from goal-post	✓✓✓	3
Confident	✓✓✓✓	4			

Repartee with Shooters Good ✓ Poor	**Response to Defending** Good ✓ Poor **Interceptions** Total ✓✓✓ 3
Throw-ups Successful ✓ 1 Unsuccessful	**Marking Player** Good ✓ Poor **Marking Space** Good Poor ✓
Court Linkage Good ✓ Poor	**Timing** Good ✓ Poor

Fig. 157 Showing an example of charting the response by WA

between players may well show up. Even when this state has been achieved, there may still be problems for the coach, in that the 'big' match occasion causes changes in the performance level of the players. A particular player may perform ideally in practice but, when faced with an important match, may be overcome by nerves and lack of experience. The coach may find that she has to give the player more than one opportunity to take part in such matches before finally coming to any conclusion.

TEAM SELECTION CRITERIA

Other attributes become important if the players still show a common level of skill and tactical ability. It might be necessary to compare the relationship they have with their team-mates, their reactions to adverse circumstances, their resilience or response after losing a match, and of course their reaction to the physical stress of consistently hard match play. In the perfect situation the coach or selector would like to see the players under every possible circumstance before coming to a final decision, but there is seldom sufficient time or opportunity to do this.

Since netball is an amateur game, the whole process of selection tends to be done during a relatively short period of time, and some degree of change within the selected group is usually allowed so that the coach may make changes where and when appropriate. The use of objective assessment seems to be of some importance when players are seen infrequently; the more often a coach observes the player, the easier may be the decision to include or exclude that player from the team. Perhaps one of the reasons why professional football managers use subjective assessment so often is just because they are so familiar with their players and so aware of the level of performance that each player can produce.

Clearly, there are some differences between selecting a team and selecting a squad of players, since the selection of a squad suggests that a degree of improvement may be necessary for some players before they are given the opportunity to play for the team. It may well be part of the strategy to include young or inexperienced players who show definite potential, so that the group has depth. A coach who is preparing a number of players for future important occasions may be fully aware of the danger of relying too heavily on existing team members. She may be looking forward to a major competition which will demand a balance of youth and energy together with experience. She may need to provide within a squad a number of players who are capable of playing in more than one position effectively, while at the same time building a group which is cohesive in personality. What is selected for that coach may well be the direct result of her declaring her policy or strategy to the selection committee; however, such a step would imply that there is time to prepare players and that her long-term plans are achievable within the time at her disposal.

The selection of a team may be dictated by different criteria, since the players may be expected to perform well with only a few practice sessions, the main theme of those sessions being team cohesion rather than skills development. The selection of the reserves for such an occasion might demand that, while the team players can be selected for specific positions, the reserves may need to display an ability to play in a number of positions. A touring team or a team for a netball rally, which demands participation in match play over a period of time, may demand a consistency of both strength and endurance together with all the other attributes of a good games player. This demand may well cause the inclusion of some players who show resilience even under stress and fatigue, and the exclusion of others whose performance varies over a period of time, even though some of these latter players may show something 'special' at times.

Even within that group of selected players there may be times when a particular match against a team which has been well researched by the coach will call for a specific job to be done by a particular player. There may be a need to counteract the skill of a known opponent, causing a change in the team, and the tactical use of the players may become the criterion for selection by the coach.

Finally, although on balance the squad or team is mainly selected according to the performance of the players, it cannot be said that this is the only area which is important in the selection. Players who have to spend long hours in each other's company, who have to travel together, live together in strange surroundings, share accommodation and work or train together in sometimes less than perfect conditions have to withstand all these things and still rise to each demanding occasion. The need to find players who can combine both socially and within the game of netball may set yet another limitation on the freedom of choice.

SELECTION OF THE CAPTAIN

One of the major tasks of the captain is to act as liaison between the coach and the players. The task of captaincy can be made easier if she is fully aware of her responsibilities and duties. Usually a captain is selected who has had plenty of previous match experience, and who has seen her predecessor at work. However, coaches should not assume that captains know their role, and guidelines should be discussed. Figure 157 is an example of possible guidelines given by a club coach to the captains of all her teams.

Captains can be elected by all members of the squad, or they can be selected by the coach (or selection panel). Since all playing positions are determined by the coach, and since the captain must be the coach's 'right-hand man', there exists a strong argument in favour of the coach appointing the captain.

The team captain should represent the ideal model in terms of example. It may be that she is a most skilful player, but it is more important that she can take control of any situation which arises either during the match or in her dealings with the group, and that she can organise herself and the group easily. The efficient team captain should be capable of motivating her players, and in this respect she may well be regarded as necessarily a charismatic personality.

CAPTAINS

A. My right-hand man. Discuss with me:
i strengths and weaknesses of your players
ii team combinations
iii promotions/demotions
iv tactical ideas/patterns of play. Liaise with one another — main discussion (time for all of us) prior to weekly training sessions

B. You are the leader of your team:
i know your players' problems (which affect play and/or attendance)
ii keep morale high
iii look after *all* your players

C. Set the example/standards in:
i play (match and practice)
ii behaviour (on and off court)
iii appearance
iv attitude

D. Responsible at matches for:
i bibs, ball, posts/nets, etc.
ii refreshments/oranges, etc.
iii providing the umpire
iv tossing for ends, three cheers for opponents and umpires
v checking the scorecards and posting to league secretary
vi giving results to publicity officer
vii checking the changing room is left clean

E. Keep records of: (record book is provided)
i attendance at practices (L for late!)
ii matches and position played
iii score
iv umpire (and his/her expenses)

F. Responsible at practices to see someone helps:
i collect in bibs and balls
ii reinforce the club notices

Fig. 158 Possible guidelines for club captains

The captain in the club team, while being 'one of the girls', will usually have much experience in her sport, and should reflect that knowledge to her players by demonstrating her skill consistently and often almost quietly. She does not need to be ostentatious: her ability should be obvious. Her willingness, often off the court, to do the ordinary day-to-day tasks as well as the more attractive tasks of the captaincy should be recognised by her players and should, hopefully, demand a degree of respect from them and from the coach.

The practical tasks, such as tossing the coin to determine first centre pass, calling the team together to cheer the opposition (and the umpires?),or thanking the umpires and all other officials, are straightforward. The behind-the-scenes work of the captain can place a heavy demand on her in terms of time and effort, so care should be taken to select a player whose own playing performance will not be adversely affected by her assuming so much additional responsibility.

The captain is the leader of the group of players and, while she will be aware of the importance of the team as a unit, she must also be prepared to give time to the individual members and be a willing listener. She should be aware of what constitutes a real problem and of what is perhaps only a small problem which she can solve without going to her coach or manager. Her concern and caring for her individual team or squad members should always be paramount.

Knowing that she has to relate good news, such as the inclusion of players in the team, as well as bad news, such as exclusion, the captain needs to be tactful and understanding, while at the same time maintaining an objective view of the long- and short-term aims of the coach. She has to be confident in her own judgement and in that of her coach, and at the same time see that justice is done. A captain will need to discuss, confidentially, about players' performances with the coach. She should also be concerned with developing her own and her team's allegiance to the club, county, region or country which they represent.

Her ability to address both the team and the supporters with ease is important, since she could be called upon to speak with sincerity in public. The ability to speak with *humour* is not essential, but it is interesting to note that many captains can amuse as well as convey a message.

Coaches and captains have to be able to work amicably together, each one fully supporting the other. Coaches should not overload captains with onerous tasks, nor should they appoint a captain without offering opportunities for her to develop her leadership role. A captain should know clearly what is expected of her, and as a result should be confident in her team, her coach, her own playing performance and her role as captain.

Captaincy should be a joy and an honour.

Bibliography

4 Progressing skills into tactics

Brown, Joyce *Netball the Australian Way*, Victoria (Australia), Stone and Mill, 1978

Cousy, Bob, and Power, Frank *Basketball Concepts and Techniques*, Boston, Allyn and Bacon, 1970

Cratty, Bryant J. *Psychology and Physical Activity*, Englewood Cliffs (NJ), Prentice-Hall, 1968

Dewhurst-Hands, Sally *Netball – A Tactical Approach*, London, Faber and Faber, 1980

Wade, Alan *The F.A. Guide to Training and Coaching*, London, Heinemann, 1967

Wein, Horst *The Science of Hockey*, London, Pelham Books, 1979

6 Planning a coaching programme

Beutelstahl, D. *Volleyball, Play to Win*, London, Ward Lock, 1978

Churchman, C. West *The Systems Approach*, New York, De La Courte Press, 1968

Coaching Association of Canada *Sports Science Periodical Research and Technology in Sport*, April, 1981

Grayson, E. *Sport and the Law*, London, *Sunday Telegraph* Publications, September, 1978

LaPoint, James D. *Organisation and Management of Sport*, Iowa, Kendal Hunt Publishing, 1980

Reddin, W.J. *Effective MBO*, New York, McGraw-Hill, 1983

7 Physiological considerations

Astrand, P.O., and Rodahl, K. *Textbook of Work Physiology*, New York, McGraw-Hill, 1970

Brouha, L. 'Training', chapter in Johnson, W.R. (Editor), *Science and Medicine of Exercise and Sports*, New York, Harper and Brothers, 1960

De Vries, H.A. *Physiology of Exercise*, London, Staples Press, 1967

Edington, D.W., and Edgerton, V.R. *The Biology of Physical Activity*, Boston, Houghton Mifflin, 1976

Klafs, C.E., and Lyons, M.J. *Female Athlete: A Coach's Guide to Conditioning and Training*, St Louis, C.V. Mosby Co., 1976

Morehouse, and Miller, A.T. *Physiology of Exercise* (7th Edition), St Louis, C.V. Mosby Co., 1976

Wilmore, J.H. *Athletic Training and Physical Fitness*, Boston, Allyn and Bacon, 1976

Wright, S. *Applied Physiology* (12th Edition), r.e. C.A. Keele, Oxford Medical Publications, 1978

8 The contribution of sports psychology to netball

Alderman, R.B. *Psychological Behaviour in Sport*, Philadelphia, W.B. Saunders, 1974

Butt, D.S. 'What Can Psychology Offer to the Athlete and the Coach?', in Suinn, R.M. (Editor), *Psychology in Sports: Methods and Applications*, Minneapolis, Burgess Publishing Co., 1980

Kirby, R., and Radford, J. *Individual Differences*, London, Methuen, 1976

Klavora, P., and Daniel, J.V. *Coach, Athlete and the Sport Psychologist*, Toronto, Human Kinetics Publishers, 1979

Musson, P.H., Conger, J.J., and Kagen, J. *Child Development and Personality*, New York, Harper and Row, 1979

Schmidt, R.A. *Motor Skills*, New York, Harper and Row, 1975

Singer, R.N. *Coaching, Athletics and Psychology*, New York, McGraw-Hill, 1971

Singer, R.N. 'Sports Psychology: An Introduction', in Straub, W.F. (Editor), *Sports Psychology: An Analysis of Athletic Behaviour*, New York, Mouvement Publications, 1978

Straub, W. F. (Editor) *Sports Psychology: An Analysis of Athletic Behaviour*, New York, Mouvement Publications, 1978

Suinn, R.M. (Editor) *Psychology in Sports: Methods and Applications*, Minneapolis, Burgess Publishing Co., 1980

9 Diet and nutrition

Paish, Wilf *Diet in Sport*, A & C Black, 1989

10 The application of biomechanics to netball skills

Daish, C.H. *The Physics of Ball Games*, London, Hodder and Stoughton, 1972

Dyson, G.H.G. *The Mechanics of Athletics*, London, Hodder and Stoughton, 1977

Hay, J.G. *The Biomechanics of Sports Techniques*, Englewood Cliffs (NJ), Prentice-Hall, 1973

Page, R.L. *The Physics of Human Movement*, Exeter, Wheaton, 1978

12 Measurement and evaluation in netball

Allard, F., and Starkes, J.L. 'Perception in Sport: Volleyball', *Journal of Sport Psychology*, 2.1, 22 – 33 (1980)

Allison, B. 'A Practical Application of Specificity in Netball Training', *Sports Coach*, 2.2, 9 – 12 (1978)

Barham, P.J. 'A Systematic Analysis of Play in Netball', *Sports Coach*, 4.2, 27 – 31 (1980)

Barham, P.J., and Wilson, N.C. 'Skill and Fitness Assessment of Netball Players', *Sports Coach*, 5.3, 20 – 24 (1981)

Battles, J., and Odom, C.J. 'Predictor Variables: A Consideration for Coaches', *Journal of Physical Education, Recreation and Dance*, May 1982, 11 – 12

Embrey, L. 'Analysing Netball Matches', *Sports Coach*, 2.3, 35 – 37 (1978)

Knowles, J.E., and Brooke, J.D. 'A Movement Analysis of Player Behaviour in Soccer Match Performance', Salford, *BSSP Conference Papers*, 1974

Miller, B.P. 'Tests and Measurement in the Assessment of Athletic Ability', *Circle*, 21, 14 – 15 (1982)

Miller, B.P. 'Visual Factors in Netball Performance: Theory into Practice', forthcoming

Parker, H. 'Current Games Research: Skill Testing in Netball', *Sports Coach*, 1.3, 10 – 14 (1977)

Parker, H. 'Visual Detection and Perception in Netball', in Cockerill, I.M., and MacGillivary, W.W. (Editors), *Vision and Sport*, Cheltenham, Stanley Thornes, 1981

Reilly, T., and Thomas, V. 'A Motion Analysis of Work-Rate in Different Positional Roles in Professional Football Match-Play', *Journal of Human Movement Studies*, 2, 87 – 97 (1976)

Index